ARAMAIC LIGHT ON THE ACTS OF THE APOSTLES

Aramaic New Testament Series
Volume 4

Books in print by Rocco A. Errico

Setting A Trap for God: The Aramaic Prayer of Jesus
Let There Be Light: The Seven Keys
And There Was Light
The Mysteries of Creation: The Genesis Story
The Message of Matthew: An Annotated Parallel Aramaic-English Gospel of Matthew
Classical Aramaic – Book 1

Spanish publication
La Antigua Oración Aramea de Jesus: El Padrenuestro

German publications
Acht Einstimmungen auf Gott: Vaterunser
Es Werde Licht

Books in print by Rocco A. Errico and George M. Lamsa
Aramaic New Testament Series: Volumes 1 – 4
Aramaic Light on the Gospel of Matthew
Aramaic Light on the Gospels of Mark and Luke
Aramaic Light on the Gospel of John
Aramaic Light on the Acts of the Apostles

Books in print by George M. Lamsa
The Holy Bible from the Ancient Eastern Text
New Testament Origin
The Shepherd of All – The 23rd Psalm
The Kingdom on Earth
Idioms in the Bible Explained & A Key to the Original Gospels

ARAMAIC LIGHT ON THE ACTS OF THE APOSTLES

A commentary based on Aramaic, the language of Jesus, and ancient Near Eastern customs

Aramaic New Testament Series
Volume 4

Rocco A. Errico / George M. Lamsa

The Noohra Foundation, Inc
Smyrna, Georgia

Aramaic Light on the Acts of the Apostles—copyright © 2003 by Rocco A. Errico. All rights reserved. Printed in the United States of America. No part of this book may be used or reproduced in any manner whatsoever without written permission except in the case of brief quotations embodied in critical articles and reviews. For information, address Noohra Foundation, 4480H South Cobb Drive SE, PMB343, Smyrna Georgia 30080, E-mail: noohrafnd@aol.com.

First Printing December 2003

ISBN: 0-9631292-9-5

The Lamsa translation quotations in this book are reprinted by permission of Harper Collins, Publishers, Inc., from the *Holy Bible from the Ancient Eastern Text,* George M. Lamsa's translation from the Aramaic of the Peshitta. Copyright 1933; renewed 1961 by Nina Shabaz. Copyright 1939; renewed 1967 by Nina Shabaz. Copyright 1940; renewed 1968 by Nina Shabaz. Copyright 1957 by Nina Shabaz.

Our most sincere and heartfelt thanks to

Mrs. Donalyn Kling

whose generosity and love of the knowledge of truth

made the publication of this commentary possible

CONTENTS

Foreword by Rocco A. Errico ix

Introduction by Rocco A. Errico and George M. Lamsa xi

Abbreviations xviii

THE COMMENTARY

Introduction: *The Acts of the Apostles* 1

Chapter 1 3

Chapter 2 18

Chapter 3 34

Chapter 4 39

Chapter 5 47

Chapter 6 54

Chapter 7 61

Chapter 8 73

Chapter 9 84

Chapter 10 93

Chapter 11 104

Chapter 12 108

Chapter 13 114

Chapter 14 120

Chapter 15 130

Chapter 16 138

Chapter 17 149

Chapter 18 158

Chapter 19 165

Chapter 20 176

Chapter 21 186

Chapter 22 194

Chapter 23 199

Chapter 24 203

Chapter 25 (no comments in this chapter) ....

Chapter 26 205

Chapter 27 208

Chapter 28 211

Bibliography 217

About the Author—George M. Lamsa 219

About the Author—Rocco A. Errico 221

FOREWORD
by Rocco A. Errico

Aramaic Light on the Acts of the Apostles, New Testament Series Volume 4, continues in the same arrangement as the preceding commentaries—*Aramaic Light on the Gospel of Matthew, Aramaic Light on the Gospels of Mark and Luke,* and *Aramaic Light on the Gospel of John.* This volume acts as a Near Eastern guide, revealing to the Western mind a more intimate view of the socio-religious and psychological environment of the time. It presents the outworking of the apostles in its ancient Semitic culture and the atmosphere in which the Church came into existence after the crucifixion and resurrection of Jesus of Nazareth.

FORMATION OF THIS COMMENTARY

This work is not a verse by verse commentary. The comments are to serve the reader in understanding the Near Eastern language, peoples and times. It is not founded on contemporary academic analysis of Scripture, nor does it actively employ critical source/ historical and literary methods of interpretation. Nonetheless, on certain passages, I do make a few references to some of these findings in the footnotes. As much as possible, each comment is written in story form, using layman's language and not theological, specialized terminology. This style is maintained throughout the volume.

All scriptural excerpts at the beginning of each comment are from the King James Version of the New Testament. The comments also contain quotes of scriptural passages from *The Holy Bible from Ancient Eastern Manuscripts* by Dr. George M. Lamsa. These quotations are identified as the "Aramaic Peshitta text, Lamsa translation." There are other citations of Scripture in the body of the comments that I have translated directly from the Aramaic Peshitta text. These passages are identified as "Aramaic Peshitta text, Errico."

I have attempted as much as possible to avoid a collision with denominational belief systems and interpretations as well as various schools of systematic theological studies. Nevertheless, in certain scriptural passages cited in this volume, it became unavoidable. Apparently some biblical interpreters have unwittingly created and established monumental dogmas and confusing notions on verses that were only Semitic idiomatic phrases, metaphoric expressions or biblical customs.

ACKNOWLEDGMENTS AND FINAL WORD

My deep appreciation and sincere gratitude to Mr. David Shabaz and family, as proprietors of the Lamsa estate, for their kind and most gracious permission to edit, revise, expand, annotate and prepare Dr. Lamsa's previous commentaries, *New Testament Commentary* and *More Light on the Gospel*, in a new format. I have also added material that Dr. Lamsa and I had only drafted before he passed from this earthly life on September 22, 1975 as well as information derived from my continual research in Aramaic word meanings and Near Eastern studies.

My very genuine and heartfelt thanks and gratefulness to Ms. Sue Edwards, Mrs. Ann Milbourn, Ms. Linetta Izenman and Mr. Hanny Freiwat for their constructive suggestions and assistance in preparing this manuscript for publication. In addition, the board of the Noohra Foundation and I are extremely grateful to Mrs. Donalyn Kling, whose generosity and devotion and dedication to the Aramaic work made the publication of this work possible.

To all readers of this commentary, I say to you: *taybootha washlama dalaha nehwoon amhon hasha walmeen!* "The grace (loving kindness) and peace of God are with you now and always!"

Rocco A. Errico
November 14, 2003

INTRODUCTION

THE NEW TESTAMENT

New Testament writings, like those of the Hebrew Scriptures, were handed down in scrolls. Sections of these writings were in the possession of churches and individuals for many years. For example, the gospel of Matthew was originally written on several scrolls, probably five or six. Years later those scrolls were arranged and compiled into a single narrative that came to be known as the Gospel according to St. Matthew. The compilation of Scripture began in the second century, but writing on scrolls never ceased. In the Near East today one can find portions of Scripture on scrolls. A few complete texts of the Old and New Testaments have been found compiled together.

The four gospels were handed down in single volumes. The book of Acts circulated as a single document. Pauline epistles were grouped and bound together. There were, however, some texts in which the four gospels and the remainder of the New Testament writings, with the exception of the book of the Revelation and a few minor epistles, were bound together.

The gospels of Matthew, Mark, Luke and John contain the teachings of Jesus. The book of Acts is the history of the early Church, its growth and expansion. Paul's letters and the general epistles are based on the teachings of Jesus. In other words, these writings, the epistles, are commentaries and expositions on the teachings of Jesus. Therefore, the reader must distinguish between Jesus' teachings and the writings about his teachings by his disciples and their disciples and followers.

THE TEACHINGS OF JESUS

Jesus' teachings are authoritative; that is, they are based on his infinite, spiritual understanding of God, humanity and religion. Jesus spoke with direct authority and did not quote other teachers or traditions to confirm or affirm what he taught. His teachings were not from men but from his own spiritual genius, which we call God.

In his sayings and discourses, Jesus touched on the Torah and the prophets. He did this to some extent so that he might explain to the Jewish religious authorities and the people the spiritual meaning behind these sacred writings. In some instances what he said was already written in the books of the prophets. One could easily say that the Hebrew prophets gave the formulas that could cure the ills that plague humanity. But Jesus was like a great chemist who knew how to mix those formulas and produce the healing elixir for humankind. He had the power and inner understanding to interpret holy Scripture, reveal the mysteries that they contained and to write a new, higher law—a law that was to be written on human hearts and not on stone tablets or sheepskins.

Jesus' mind was free from complicated, religious doctrines and traditions that hampered truth and closed the door of God's kingdom. His teachings were based on divine inspiration. Palestinians of his day were moved and impressed when they heard him preach and debate with the Pharisees and Sadducees. "And the Jews marveled saying, How does this man know how to read, when he has not been instructed? Jesus answered and said, My teaching is not mine, but his who sent me."[1]

THE WRITINGS OF THE APOSTLES

The apostles and their disciples were born and reared in Judaism. They were greatly influenced by their cultural religious traditions, customs and interpretation of the Torah based on the elders. For a long time, they were unable to understand fully the teachings of their Master. They also could not divorce themselves completely from the

---

[1] Jn. 7:15-16., Aramaic Peshitta text, Lamsa translation.

religious background that had nurtured them. They would often fall back on the interpretations of Scripture from their past learning.

In their writings and preaching, the apostles relied on Hebrew Scripture, Jewish history, and the Mosaic laws and ordinances. Jesus, in his preaching, never told his followers whether to circumcise or not. He never recommended Jewish temple ceremonies, the system of priesthood, food laws, and many other matters, some of which became the center of controversies during the apostolic period. Jesus never claimed ties with any royal family. What he taught had its own authority and did not need a special, royal blood line behind it.

For many years, the apostles and their Jewish followers remained faithfully in the bosom of the Judaism of their time. They prayed in the temple, fasted, observed the Sabbath Day, circumcised their male children, made vows and shaved (had their hair cut) in the temple, and abstained from eating certain meats and avoided bloody meats.

THE PRESENT NEW TESTAMENT CANON

The New Testament in its present form is what survived from the apostolic writings. Some sections of Scripture were lost and others perished during the persecution that began in the first century after Jesus and lasted to the fourth century. Some writings were rejected when an approved and common New Testament canon was formed after the Nicene Council in 325 CE. Evidently some of these rejected writings were forged; others were probably contrary to the new teachings and dogmas.

Undoubtedly many manuscripts containing the writings of other apostles were lost. Thaddeus,[2] Thomas and Peter were the evangelizers of Mesopotamia, Persia, and India and founders of the ancient Church of the East. Millions of Christians in Malabar, India,

---

[2] Mt. 10:3.

carry St. Thomas' name. Simon Peter preached in Babylon.[3] In our New Testament canon we have only the writings of four apostles who had been with Jesus: Matthew, John, James (Jacob) and Peter. However, modern New Testament scholars believe that we have no writing from any of the apostles.

THE EPISTLES

The epistles were pastoral letters addressed to congregations in various parts of the Roman Empire. Their purpose was to admonish, teach and strengthen the converts. The writers probably never thought that their writings would survive and become sacred literature. (Although many of these writings were lost or destroyed, it is a miracle that so many of them have survived to the present day.)

DATING OF NEW TESTAMENT BOOKS

Not one of the books of the New Testament was dated by the apostles or scribes. Therefore, all dates given to the different books and epistles are conjectural.

In biblical days and until not too long ago, documents, birth records, contracts, and legal papers were dated from the years of certain kings, wars, famines and other important events. This is still the custom in many remote Near Eastern regions where birth and death records are not kept. For example, the birth of a prominent man was usually based on the year in which a certain king ascended the throne or a certain leader came into power, but in some instances we have no accurate way to ascertain the year.

In those days, each nation had its own way of reckoning time. Calendars were known but not universally adopted. Therefore, the only thing all the scribes could do when dating their writings was to

---

[3] 1 Peter 5:13.

mention the year of the reigning king. Some of the scribes did not even take the trouble to practice this form of dating. The reason for this is that Scriptures were primarily written for instruction, discipline and consolation. Both writers and readers were interested only in the message and the person of Jesus.

DATING CHALLENGES

The beginning of the Christian movement actually has no positive date. It is commonly calculated from an incorrect starting point. It begins with the reign of Herod, who is supposed to have been made King of Judea in the year 40 BCE, and died in the thirty-seventh year of his reign. Jesus' birth is thought to have occurred in 4 BCE.

The practice of dating from "the year of our Lord" began in the sixth century when Dionysius Exiguus made the year of Jesus' birth correspond to the Roman year 754. However, Near Easterners dated some of their manuscripts from the Greek conquest of Asia—that is, 311 BCE. This practice continued until the sixteenth century, as is seen from Aramaic manuscripts.

It makes little difference what year Jesus was born or how old he was when he died on the cross. It is important, however, to have a plausible reckoning of time and events beginning from the ascension of Jesus. This will give us some light on the growth and expansion of the movement under the guidance of the apostles and the period in which the New Testament was written.

One must realize that considerable periods of time elapsed between Jesus' death, the establishment of churches in Judea and Syria, and Paul's conversion to the new movement. These churches were not organized overnight. It took many years before the disciples and followers of Jesus separated themselves from the Jewish synagogues and began organizing and establishing congregations of their own. In the book of Acts we are told that Paul persecuted Jesus' disciples and followers in Judea and Syria.[4]

PAUL AND CHRISTIANITY

Paul, Mark and Luke had never seen Jesus. When they embraced Jesus' gospel and became adherents to his teachings, only some of the apostles were still living. Had these men been with Jesus they would have mentioned it. Paul, in all of his writings, never makes any reference to having seen Jesus before his death. Yet he was a learned man and a member of the Jewish faith and council.

Had he been living during Jesus' lifetime, Paul would have seen him and would have mentioned something about Jesus' arrest, trial, and the opposition of the Sanhedrin. He would have had access to Jewish documents and other information concerning Jesus' death. But the event had occurred long before, so much so that Jewish records concerning Jesus had perished. Paul, throughout his missionary journeys, basically preached Jesus' gospel of the kingdom.[5]

When Paul was a young man, the Christian movement was already organized, rivaling Judaism. When Stephen was stoned, Paul was guarding the clothes of the men who participated in his murder.[6] Thus, we must realize that there was a long period of time between Jesus and Paul and between Jewish and Gentile Christianity.

AN IMPORTANT NOTE: THE TERM "SEMITIC"

When the terms "Semitic" and "Semite" are used in this commentary, they refer to behavior or beliefs that apply both to Near Eastern Jews who kept the customs and manners of the ancient Middle East as well as to all other Semitic peoples, such as

---

[4] Acts 9:1-4.
[5] Rom 15:19; Acts 28: 30-31.
[6] Acts 7:58.

Assyrians, Syrians (Arameans), Chaldeans, Arabs and other Semitic races. (These terms do not apply to Westernized Semitic peoples.) The original spelling of "Semite" was "Shemite," which derives from Shem, one of the sons of Noah.

Rocco A. Errico and George M. Lamsa

ABBREVIATIONS

Old Testament

Gen.	Genesis
Ex.	Exodus
Lev.	Leviticus
Num.	Numbers
Dt.	Deuteronomy
1 Sam.	1 Samuel
2 Sam.	2 Samuel
1 Ki.	1 Kings
2 Ki.	2 Kings
2 Chron.	2 Chronicles
Ps.	Psalms
Isa.	Isaiah
Jer.	Jeremiah
Ezk.	Ezekiel

New Testament

Mt.	Matthew
Mk.	Mark
Lk.	Luke
Jn.	John
Rom.	Romans
1 Cor.	1 Corinthians
2 Cor.	2 Corinthians
Gal.	Galatians
Eph.	Ephesians
Col.	Colossians
1 Tim.	1 Timothy
Tit.	Titus
Heb.	Hebrews
Rev.	Revelation

Other Abbreviations

BCE	Before the common era, BC
CE	Common Era, AD
K.J.V.	King James Version

ܟܬܒܐ

ܕܦܘܫܩܐ ܕܙܠܡܬܐ܇

ܠܡܪܝ ܒܗܢܡ܂

INTRODUCTION
The Acts of the Apostles

THE BOOK

The book of Acts is an account of the early Christian movement. It begins with the ascension of Jesus into heaven, the descent of the Holy Spirit, and then describes the apostolic ministry. At the Jewish feast of Pentecost, the disciples and followers of Jesus organized the movement in Jerusalem; from there they started their worldwide work.

The author of the book is Luke, who is also the author of the third synoptic gospel that bears his name. The Christian historian Eusebius tells us that Luke was a Syrian from Antioch. Luke presents a record of the Judean church and its activities, the persecution of the apostles and their followers, the murder of Jacob (James), son of Zebedee, the martyrdom of Stephen, Saul's conversion and his later missionary endeavors, and the first church council in Jerusalem.

LUKE AND PAUL

A large portion of the book is devoted to the work of Paul and his ministry throughout Judea, Asia Minor, Greece, and Rome. This new spiritual movement began its expansion from Palestine and flowed into other parts of the world. Because of the persecutions in the holy city, Antioch replaced Jerusalem as the main headquarters of the movement. It became the greatest evangelizing center for the spread of Jesus' gospel of God's kingdom.

Luke accompanied Paul on many of his missionary journeys. When Luke was not traveling with him, he refers to Paul and his companions as "them" and "they." When he was with Paul on his mission work, Luke uses "we." The author keeps himself in the background. He does not disclose any of his own activities, but he does record most of the important events. Luke's narratives include healing episodes and miraculous escapes from prisons. These stories are woven around discourses and speeches.

THE DATING OF THE BOOK

The precise date for this writing, like that of the four gospels, is not known. It may have been written about 70 CE.[1] It is most probable that the first part of the book of Acts was written prior to the conversion of Paul. Luke gathered some of his material from the apostles and eyewitnesses, since he was a later convert to the movement. (It is believed that he was a third generation believer.)

For example, Luke was not present when Peter gave his famous address to the multitudes attending the feast of Pentecost.[2] So he freely composed his account based on the tradition that he had received from those who were present. Therefore, Peter's speech is a Lucan composition with a general sense of what was actually said.

This commentary on the book of Acts does not present a critical source/historical/literary/academic analysis or study. As always the comments are based on the Aramaic Peshitta text, language and word meanings and on ancient Near Eastern customs. These old customs and manners are slowly disappearing and gradually being replaced by modern forms of behavior and thinking. This fact alone makes the commentary extremely valuable and insightful.

---

[1] A majority of modern New Testament scholars date the book circa 85 CE give or take five or ten years. There are a few biblical authorities who think it was written in the early 60s and others in the early 100s.

[2] Acts 2:14-36.

CHAPTER 1

THE AUTHOR

The former treatise have I made, O Theophilus, of all that Jesus began both to do and teach. Acts 1:1.

Luke is considered to be the author of the third canonical gospel. His writing is titled *The Gospel of Luke* which was his "former treatise." However, the title in Aramaic reads: *Karozootha d'Luqa*, "The Preaching of Luke." This title implies that a scribe, some time later, had edited Luke's gospel and probably added or omitted other material.

Luke's purpose in his gospel writing was to set in order the teachings and works of Jesus and the narratives that he had gathered from eyewitnesses who were familiar with those events. Luke was not one of the twelve apostles nor had he ever heard Jesus teach. He was a later convert who became a companion to Paul on several missionary journeys.

The third gospel, therefore, is based on documentary evidence plus information that Luke collected from some early followers of Jesus. The birth and genealogy of Jesus and other stories about his early childhood had to be told by men and women who had known Jesus and his mother and father, Mary and Joseph. However, in his teaching and public ministry, Jesus never said anything about his ancestry or unusual conception.[1]

Apparently, Theophilus had asked Luke to write an account of the works of the apostles and the conversion of the Gentiles. In his first exposition, Luke had written about the teaching of Jesus from his

---

[1] This same thought holds true for the genealogy and nativity of Jesus, the coming of the magi and other stories in the Gospel of Matthew. See Errico and Lamsa, *Aramaic Light on the Gospel of Matthew,* "The Infancy Narrative," p. 7 and "The Ancestry of Jesus," p. 8.

birth to his ascension. Now he begins the book of Acts where he had left off in his gospel.[2]

FORTY DAYS

To whom also he shewed himself alive after his passion by many infallible proofs, being seen of them forty days, and speaking of the things pertaining to the kingdom of God. Acts 1:3.

Biblical writers frequently use the number forty in Scripture. Some Semites[3] refer to it as a sacred number. When the number is divided by ten, the result is four. This suggests the four corners of the earth, the four winds, and of course the four canonical gospels. Forty is symbolic of transformation and completeness. Both numbers twelve and forty are closely associated with the calendar and sacred Near Eastern traditions

During the time of Noah and the great flood, the rains lasted forty days and nights.[4] Moses was forty years of age when he fled from Egypt. He spent forty years in the desert as a shepherd, and while on Mount Sinai, he fasted forty days and nights.[5] Moses spent forty years in the desert traveling with the Israelites. Elijah also fasted forty days. Jewish women purified themselves forty days after childbirth.[6] Jesus' time of fasting lasted forty days and nights.[7]

According to Luke, the risen Christ spent forty days preaching, teaching and revealing certain matters to his disciples and followers concerning God's kingdom. In other words, they began to perceive and understand Jesus' message about God's spiritual kingdom. The

---

[2]For details about Luke and Theophilus, see Errico and Lamsa, *Aramaic Light on the Gospels of Mark and Luke,* "Authorship," pp. 107-108, "Luke and Theophilus," pp. 110-113.

[3]See Introduction, "An Important Note: The Term "Semitic," p. xiv-xv.

[4]Gen. 7:4.

[5]Ex. 24:18.

[6]Lk. 2:22.

[7]Mt. 4:2.

dreams of a political kingdom had been shattered by Jesus' death on the cross. His disciples had to be taught a different meaning of the messianic kingdom. Now they could reason spiritually and understand things from a new perspective.

In their eyes, Jesus' political mission had failed, but through his resurrection, he had conquered negative forces that opposed him and triumphed over death. His disciples, while grieving over the loss of their master and teacher, began to rise in consciousness and became convinced of his spiritual mission and the unseen kingdom that was soon to become a reality for them.

Nevertheless, some of his disciples were still thinking of the Davidic kingdom and were hoping for another attempt to restore political power to Israel. But Jesus told them that it was not for them to know the times or the season for such events.[8] He dismissed the question just as he had done on other occasions prior to his death.[9]

Forty days were needed to confirm his disciples' faith and explain to them matters that they had misunderstood. They had expected the restoration of the kingdom during his life on earth.[10] Jesus had to prove to them that the Messiah/Christ must suffer so that he could enter into his glory.[11]

It took forty days for the disciples to forget the political ideas about the kingdom and learn to think in terms of a spiritual messianic realm, a realm of truth. According to the written record, throughout these forty days, Jesus appeared eleven times to his disciples and followers. During this period, he was strengthening their faith in his gospel of the kingdom that he had entrusted to them.

ISRAEL'S RESTORATION

When they therefore were come together, they asked of him, saying,

---

[8] See Acts 1:7 and the comment on Acts 1:6.
[9] See Mk. 13:32.
[10] Lk. 24:21.
[11] See Lk. 24:26.

Lord, wilt thou at this time restore again the kingdom to Israel? Acts 1:6.

This was a question that Jesus had refused to answer when he was teaching his apostles and disciples. Before his death, his disciples had asked him about the restoration of the Davidic kingdom and the fulfillment of the messianic prophecies as interpreted by the Pharisees and teachers of the law. "But of that day and hour knoweth no man, no, not the angels of heaven, but my Father only."[12]

As stated in the above comment, for forty days the risen Christ had opened the minds of his disciples to the spiritual meaning of the messianic rule—that is, God's kingdom. He taught them concerning the coming of the Holy Spirit, but he did not set a time for his final triumph over the nations as Messiah. They remembered that he had told them: "Then, if any man should say to you, Behold, here is the Christ or there; believe it not."[13] And again he said: "Therefore, if they should say to you, Behold, he is in the desert, do not go out; or Behold, he is in the chamber, do not believe it."[14]

This forty day period of time began to change the apostles' lives. They saw that the present kingdoms of this world must be transformed into a spiritual rule. When this fully occurs then the nations of this world will realize that their destiny is to help lift up all humanity. There will be a very high and clear insight, a vision that reveals the oneness of all human beings. Spiritually speaking, humanity is one right now; but physically, humanity and nations are seen and understood as divided. The races of the world have the capacity to demonstrate global peace and oneness if they attune to the same channel of truth for which Jesus died.

During this time, however, some of the disciples were hoping for the restoration of Israel's political regime. They were still reasoning things out in a literal and political manner. Jesus had predicted that many events had to take place between his ascension and the final

---

[12] Mt. 24:36, K. J. V.
[13] Mt. 24:23, Aramaic Peshitta text, Lamsa translation.
[14] Mt. 24:26, Aramaic Peshitta text, Lamsa translation.

outcome of the kingdom. His gospel of the kingdom had to be preached and demonstrated throughout the world before the end would come.[15]

WITNESSES TO JESUS

But ye shall receive power, after that the Holy Ghost is come upon you: and ye shall be witnesses unto me both in Jerusalem, and in all Judea, and in Samaria, and unto the uttermost part of the earth. Acts 1:8.

Part 1—REPRESENTING JESUS. The Aramaic text reads: "But when the Holy Spirit comes upon you, you shall receive power and you shall be witnesses to me both in Jerusalem and in all Judea also in the province of Samaria and to the uttermost part of the earth."[16] The risen Christ assures his apostles and disciples that when the Holy Spirit comes upon them they would have the power[17] to be witnesses to him. That is, the disciples would have the ability to represent Jesus and his gospel of the kingdom with demonstrations of the spirit to heal people spiritually, mentally, emotionally and physically. They were to continue subverting prejudice, bigotry, violence and hatred. These men and women were to cure the poisonous thoughts that create mistrust and fear of others. And because of the threat this movement represented to all established political ideologies and religious notions, these disciples would also put their lives in danger. They were to repeat the preaching, teaching and demonstrations of God's kingdom that Jesus also represented. They were truly his witnesses, beginning in Jerusalem and to the ends of the earth.

Part 2—SAMARIA. The Aramaic text reads *beth shamrayeh,* "the province of Samaria" or "Samaritan territory," not "the city of Samaria." The latter was the capital of the Northern Kingdom that

---

[15] See Mt. 24:14.
[16] Acts 1:8, Aramaic Peshitta text, Lamsa translation.
[17] The Aramaic word for "power" in this verse is *hila*, "energy"—that is, "the ability (empowerment) to perform what needs to be demonstrated."

included the Ten Tribes of Israel. The word *Shamrin*, "Samaria," sometimes was used for the city of Samaria and on other occasions for the whole state, just as we speak of New York and New York state. For instance, "Washington backs England" does not mean Washington, D.C., but the United States as a whole. Biblical writers also used the term Babylon when referring to the Chaldean Empire. In times past countries were often referred to by the names of their capitals.

Samaritan territory, in this case, means a district that was restricted to Samaritan people, just as Utah was once restricted to the Mormons. Such territories are to be found in many parts of the Near East, where members of rival sects live in seclusion, practice their religions and maintain their traditions by working and trading among themselves. For example, until the territory of the "devil worshipers" near Mosul was occupied by England, no other class of people dwelt there. They did not permit strangers to enter their territory, fearing interference with their faith. Even in a few areas today, one can hardly find followers of other faiths in their villages. This is also true of many districts in Kurdistan, Arabia, Persia (Iran), and some parts of China. The territory is restricted to the members of the respective faiths alone.

During the time of Jesus, Palestine was divided into several provinces that were governed by Tetrarchs (governors). Samaritans were given a territory in the province of Samaria. Although Galileans were racially different from the Jews, they adhered to the Jewish faith. But the Jews questioned their sincerity as true members of Judaism.[18] However, Galileans were religiously closer to the Jews although racially akin to the Samaritans. Therefore, the Samaritans hated them.

Jesus' disciples were to succeed in converting the Samaritans, who were the enemies of both Galileans and Jews. Jesus' gospel of the kingdom was to break down racial and religious barriers and to plant love in place of hatred and truth in place of traditions. The God

---

[18]See Ezra 4:1-4.

of Israel would no longer be worshiped in Mount Gerizim, nor in Jerusalem, but in the hearts of men, women and children everywhere.[19]

TAKEN UP

And when he had spoken these things, while they beheld, he was taken up; and a cloud received him out of their sight. Acts 1:9.

Part 1—CLOUDS. In times past, nomadic tribes who lived in seclusion believed that clouds were living creatures commissioned by God to perform certain duties, such as taking care of crops, supplying streams and rivers and carrying people to and from heaven. This belief was largely due to the fact that in the desert and other dry regions the clouds in motion appeared to be engaged in some purposeful activity.

When clouds were seen moving from dry areas toward the sea, people often said: "The clouds are going to the sea after water." The reason for this notion is that the clouds on their way to the sea look white and pale, but on their return they appear dark and heavy as if they were now bearing the burden of the water they had drawn from the sea.

Scripture tells us that during the reign of King Ahab a drought had occurred in Israel and that the prophet Elijah was praying from the summit of Mt. Carmel for rain. As soon as the prophet saw a cloud coming from the sea, he immediately predicted that rain was on its way. He instructed King Ahab to rush for shelter from the impending downpour.[20]

In the desert, heaven seems a very short distance from the earth and only a little above the clouds. In those days, it was customary to go up on the high places to pray and to offer sacrifices, because

---

[19]See Errico and Lamsa, *Aramaic Light on the Gospel of John,* "The Samaritans," pp. 123-125.
[20]See 1 Ki. 18:44.

people thought that those places were nearer to the throne of God. In other words, worshipers thought that they could more easily and readily get God's ear when making their petitions and supplications. In Kurdistan and other parts of the Near East some of the people still pray at ancient, sacred shrines on the tops of high mountains.

Part 2—THE ASCENSION. The concept about clouds and the sky made it easier for the early disciples and followers to believe in the ascension of their Lord. There is also an episode recorded in the gospels which says that Moses and Elijah had been seen on the Mount of Transfiguration with Jesus and that both of them, after speaking with Jesus, were taken up in a cloud. The writers of the synoptic gospels, in their account of Jesus' transfiguration, refer to an enveloping cloud about him that filled the three witnesses—Peter, Jacob (James) and John—with awe.

The ascension of Jesus was a spiritual transformation. He rose from death and was taken up into the heavenly realm in a spiritual body, free from all physical limitation. Those apostles and disciples whose spiritual vision had been strengthened by faith in Jesus had seen him alive and ascending to heaven.[21]

TWO ANGELS AND THEIR MESSAGE

And while they looked steadfastly toward heaven as he went up, behold, two men stood by them in white apparel; Which also said, Ye men of Galilee, why stand ye gazing up into heaven? This same Jesus, which is taken up from you into heaven, shall so come in like manner as ye have seen him go into heaven. Acts 1:10-11.

Part 1—ANGELS. These two men who stood by the apostles while Jesus ascended were angels. The Aramaic word for "angel" is *malakha* and means "messenger." In the Near East angels represent purity and holiness. Near Eastern Semites think of angels as free from

---

[21] Lk. 24:51. See Errico and Lamsa, *Aramaic Light on the Gospels of Mark and Luke,* "The Ascension," pp. 272-273.

human faults and imperfections. Near Eastern Christians bury their dead in white garments, symbolic of angelic perfection. No other color is permissible.

Semites usually visualize an angel as a tall, white-bearded, elderly man clad in flowing, resplendent white robes. The reason for this idea is that priests and other church dignitaries are generally old men wearing white mantles while performing their religious duties. Conversations about angels, their rank and activities are so prevalent among Semites that some men and women claim to have seen and conversed with them. According to an old belief, everyone has a guardian angel resting on the right arm to guide him or her, and a devil on the left arm to lead the person astray.

The Hebrew word *melakh*, "angel," like the Aramaic word, also means "messenger." Both words are closely related to *milka*, "counsel," and *malka,* "king." Kings act as counselors to their people. Our English word "angel" derives from the Greek *angellos*, also meaning "messenger."

According to the Bible, angels are sent on divine errands, conveying word from God to human beings. They are also called "sons of God." In Numbers 22:23, an angel is pictured as wearing a sword, and in Daniel 10:5, an angel is seen clothed in linen. Jesus told his disciples that after the resurrection people will be like angels, free from physical weakness. The knowledge of angels is supposed to be limited.[22] Angels may be present in the form of human beings.[23] Biblical writers frequently mention angels throughout Scripture. Belief in angels and spirits came to be a doctrine during and after the Babylonian captivity of the Southern Kingdom of Judah.

The usual concept of God among some Near Eastern Semites is that of an ancient, Semitic monarch dressed in costly robes, adorned with jewels, and seated on a golden throne surrounded by counselors whose advice he seems to need.[24] Some of these agents are repre-

---

[22]See 1 Pet. 1:12.
[23]Heb. 13:2.
[24]See 1 Ki. 22:19-23.

sented as executing his good purposes and some are engaged in punishing people for their sins, just as an earthly king might do.

The doctrine of angelology and demonology, to which many references are found in Scripture, is still prevalent among Near Eastern peoples, especially among the Muslims.

Part 2—GALILEANS. The disciples of Jesus, with the exception of Judas of Iscariot, were Galileans, and his followers were recruited chiefly from the region of Galilee. No doubt Jesus had some sympathizers and followers in Judea and Syria, but the center of his movement was the group of towns around the lake of Galilee.

Jesus himself was a Galilean, and he did most of his teaching and healing in Galilee. He made some journeys into Judea where he gained a number of disciples, but many of the Jewish officials opposed him. "After these things Jesus walked in Galilee: for he would not walk in Jewry, because the Jews sought to kill him."[25]

The work in Judea was much more difficult and challenging. Jerusalem was the center of the Jewish religion and culture. Jewish authorities were opposed to any reformers, especially to those coming from Galilee. They were expecting a political and economic Messiah who was to restore the kingdom of David and the reign of prosperity. Jesus disclaimed any political power. His was not a worldly kingdom. Hence the Jewish priests and scribes rejected him and delivered him into the hands of Pilate. Some of his disciples deserted him. Others were afraid to identify themselves with the new teaching. But many of his Galilean followers stood by him to the last.

This new spiritual movement had become strong in Galilee and the number of the faithful steadily increased. The work in Jerusalem became stronger only after Pentecost. Even then all the leaders of this movement were Galileans. The followers of Jesus in Antioch, Syria were called either "Galileans" or "Nazerenes" until the year 50 CE, when they assumed the title of *m'sheekheh,* literally "anointed ones," but translated as "Christians." The Jews also, when referring to Jesus

---

[25]Jn. 7:1, K. J. V. The term "Jews" in this verse refers only to certain Jewish religious leaders and not all Jews.

and his disciples, called them "Galileans."

Part 3—JESUS' RETURN. The return of Jesus will be a spiritual manifestation; that is, he will come in a spiritual body, free from all physical limitation. The messengers told his disciples that Jesus would "come in like manner as ye have seen him go into heaven." Jesus ascended in a spiritual body and would return in the same manner.[26] At that time, people's consciousness will be raised to a spiritual level, so that every eye will see nothing but good. In other words, it will be a spiritual life and a spiritual kingdom ruling on earth through the political systems of the world. It will not be done through force of arms or legislation. Jesus' counsel as a spiritual leader will be heeded and carried out.

The apostles saw Jesus' ascension with their human eyes. He appeared to them in a manner whereby they could recognize him. Another way to put it is: Jesus rose in a spiritual body, but appeared to the disciples in the way that they had known him formerly. Spirit can manifest in any form or manner. The Hebrew prophets conversed with the God of Israel in spirit and in visions.

At Jesus' return the whole world will recognize him. His kingdom will be established and the world will be ready to receive him. Jesus assured his disciples of his triumphant return (the success of his mission). But, he also told them that he would remain with them until the end, and that whenever two or three were gathered in his name, representing him, he would be there among them.[27]

THE APOSTLES RETURN TO JERUSALEM

Then returned they unto Jerusalem from the mount called Olivet, which is from Jerusalem a sabbath day's journey. And when they were come in, they went up into an upper room, where abode both Peter, and James, and John, and Andrew, Philip, and Thomas, Batholomew, and

---

[26]See the comment in this chapter: TAKEN UP, part 2—"THE ASCENSION," p. 9.

[27]See Jn. 14:3; Rev. 1:7.

Matthew, James the son of Alphaeus and Simon Zelotes, and Judas the brother of James. Acts 1:12-13.

Part 1—A SABBATH DAY'S JOURNEY. *Bethzeiteh* means "home of olives," i.e., "a place where olives grow abundantly." The Mount of Olives is just outside of Jerusalem. From it one can see many parts of Palestine, Jericho, the Jordan Valley and the desert. The Aramaic text reads "about a mile away." In this case, "a Sabbath Day's journey" means "a short distance." In ancient times, walking on the Sabbath was prohibited beyond the limits of the tabernacle. During the time of Jesus the length of the walk was from the temple grounds to the valley of Kedron.

Religious authorities determined the distance one could travel so that the Sabbath might not be broken. At that time, these authorities considered walking a leisurely act and did not regard it as work. However, if the walking were to include an errand, it would have to be judged under the Sabbath law. Thus, on the Sabbath day, the Jews ceased all their activities and spent the day resting at home and praying in the synagogue.

Part 2—AN UPPER ROOM. Most of the houses in Palestine were one story buildings, square in shape like a box. However, there were some houses with an upper room that was used for guests, meetings, and a place to rest. This room is called a *balakhana,* "upper room." Generally, inns had one or more *balakhanas* with doors and windows facing the courtyard. These rooms were usually rented to strangers or used as banquet places. Donkeys, horses and mules were tied up in the courtyard and the lower rooms were occupied by guests of poorer class. A few of these ancient inns still exist in Palestine, Syria and other areas of the Near East.

This upper room was probably the place where Jesus and his disciples ate the Last Supper.[28] After the resurrection Jesus appeared to them at the same place. His disciples had also been there on other occasions. They had no other place to gather. The inn was patronized

---

[28]Mk. 14:15.

by strangers who had no relatives or friends in Jerusalem.

Inns were also a good place for meeting people, receiving news and doing business. The disciples undoubtedly met merchants and converts who came down from Galilee. Also, there were a number of men and women followers of Jesus along with his mother, Mary, and probably other relatives present at the upper room. Jesus had instructed them to remain in Jerusalem until the feast of Pentecost.[29] The members of this peculiar group would have been unwelcome in the homes of people who had seen their leader die on the cross.

JUDAH'S FATE

Now this man purchased a field with the reward of iniquity; and falling headlong, he burst asunder in the midst and all his bowels gushed out. And it was known unto all the dwellers at Jerusalem; insomuch as that field is called in their proper tongue, Aceldama, that is to say, The field of blood. For it is written in the book of Psalms, Let his habitation be desolate and let no man dwell therein; and his bishoprick let another take.
Acts 1:18-20.

Part 1—THE PRICE OF SIN. The Aramaic text reads: "He is the one who earned for himself a field with the price of sin; and falling headlong, he burst open in the midst, and all his bowels gushed out."[30] In the Near East, properties are named for the person who was responsible for purchasing it. This plot was called Judas' field because it was acquired with the sinful money that he had gained from betraying his master to the religious authorities. Judas did not buy the plot or field himself.

Jewish authorities could not use the returned blood money for temple purposes so instead they purchased a small burial ground for strangers. (In the Near East strangers, especially members of rival faiths, are buried by themselves.)

---

[29] See Acts 1:4.
[30] Acts 1:18, Aramaic Peshitta text, Lamsa translation.

What probably happened was this: Once Judas fully realized what he had done to his master and how sinful his act of betrayal was, he returned the money to the priests. Then, feeling extremely remorseful, he hanged himself. It is most likely that the rope broke and he fell on some rocky ground that cut his body open. Ropes often break when heavy people are hanged.

Part 2—THE FIELD OF BLOOD. The Aramaic words in the text read: "*hqal-dema*, which is to say, *Qoryath-dem*—the field of blood." In his address, Peter renders the name of the field from one Aramaic dialect into another—that is, northern and southern dialects. There were many Jews and Galileans who spoke both dialects among the people who had come to Jerusalem on the day of Pentecost. However, there were some who spoke their native dialect only. Peter had traveled for three years with Jesus in Judea, Syria and other parts of Palestine and was able to speak in several Aramaic dialects.

Most Easterners would refuse to receive money paid as compensation for the murder of a relative. They call it "blood money." Therefore the burial ground was named the "field of blood."

Part 3—THE VACANT POSITION. In verse 20 the term "bishopric" is not quite correct. The Aramaic word *tishmishteh* means "duty or ministry." "Bishopric" was used later.

A bishop is an overseer, one who looks after ministers and their congregations. Judas was a disciple and not an overseer. While traveling with Jesus he looked after the money. He was the treasurer who later became a greedy purser and sold his master for thirty pieces of silver. When Mary of Magdala anointed Jesus' head with precious oil, Judas became angry. He thought that the oil had been wasted. He would rather have sold it for cash.[31]

Verse 20 is a quote from Psalm 109:8. When a disciple or servant is dismissed, his duty is given to another. Jesus had named Judas to a high office, but he proved to be unworthy. The vacancy created by his betrayal had to be filled by one who would be worthy of carrying out apostleship. The one chosen would become one of the

---

[31] Jn. 12:5-6.

shepherds of the great flock and a witness of the risen Christ who lives forever.

LOTS

And they gave forth their lots; and the lot fell upon Matthias; and he was numbered with the eleven apostles. Acts 1:26.

Casting lots is an ancient Near Eastern custom that is still in use in some areas of Palestine, the Arabian desert and other Near and Middle Eastern countries. Land, sheep, fish and other things are divided by casting lots. This method is considered the most honest way by which property can be divided and men elected to offices. It eliminates the possibility of bribery, discrimination or intimidation.

Biblical Israel used this method also. When Saul was selected as King of Israel, Samuel ordered lots to be cast first on the tribes, then on the families. Saul was elected by lot.[32]

When articles are to be divided, each person selects and marks a small stone or piece of wood. Then a boy or a stranger is called to place one of the stones on each article or group of articles. When the casting of lots is finished, everyone is satisfied with his lot and there are no complaints. Semites believe God intervenes and decides the issue.

The Apostles appointed two men who had seen Jesus and heard him preach and teach: Joseph called Barsabas, who was surnamed Justus, and Matthias. The latter was chosen and elected as a successor to Judas of Iscariot and was counted among the apostles. The number twelve, like seven and forty, was sacred and the apostles wished to preserve their original number.

---

[32] 1 Sam. 10:20-21.

CHAPTER 2

PENTECOST

And when the day of Pentecost was fully come, they were all with one accord in one place. Acts.2:1.

According to Hebrew Scripture, the Feast of Pentecost is one of the seven important Jewish feasts that God commanded Moses and the children of Israel to observe. "And the Lord spoke to Moses, saying, Speak to the children of Israel and say to them, Concerning the feasts of the Lord which you shall proclaim to be holy convocations, these are my feasts."[1]

These feasts were: the Feast of the Passover, the Unleavened Bread, the First Fruits, the Wave Offering, the Day of Atonement, the Feast of Tabernacles, and the Feast of Pentecost. "Even to the morrow after the seventh Sabbath you shall count fifty days: and you shall offer a meal offering of new wheat to the Lord."[2] The Feast of Pentecost fell during the harvest season. It was celebrated in commemoration of God's revelation to Moses on Mount Sinai.

Jesus told his disciples to wait in Jerusalem for the promised gift of the Holy Spirit that was to come on all of them. The Spirit was to be poured out upon the entire assembly of people and especially on the disciples: ". . . ye shall be baptized with the Holy Ghost not many days hence."[3] While teaching and preaching throughout Galilee, Jesus had promised to send the Holy Spirit to abide with his disciples. The spirit was to guide them in all matters and remind them of everything that he had taught them. But the Comforter was to come only after Jesus had ascended into heaven.[4]

---

[1] Lev. 23:1-2, Aramaic Peshitta text, Lamsa translation. For the complete command of the feasts see Lev. 23:1-44.

[2] Lev. 23:16, Aramaic Peshitta text, Lamsa translation.

[3] Acts 1:5, K. J. V.

[4] Jn. 14:16-17.

Until the day of Pentecost the scope of the gospel of God's kingdom was mostly limited to the Israelites, but after Pentecost the movement that Jesus had begun in Galilee was to become worldwide under the guidance of God's spirit. This new and powerful spiritual movement, through the apostles and disciples, was soon to be embraced by people of every race and creed.

THE FIRST FOLLOWERS

And there were dwelling at Jerusalem Jews, devout men, out of every nation under heaven. Now when this was noised abroad, the multitude came together, and were confounded, because that every man heard them speak in his own language. And they were all amazed and marvelled, saying one to another, Behold, are not all these which speak Galileans? Acts 2:5-7.

Part 1—JEWISH FOLLOWERS. The first followers of Jesus were all of the Jewish faith. In the beginning they were mostly Galileans, then Jews from Judea and Syria and some Samaritans. To these people the teaching of Jesus, his gospel of God's kingdom, was the fulfillment of Judaism. These followers of the Nazarene prophet worshiped in the Jewish temple and synagogues, observed the Jewish customs and traditions and kept the Mosaic law.

Jewish adherents to Jesus' teaching came from many foreign countries to the feast of the Passover and to worship at the temple, which was the national shrine and center of the Jewish faith. For many centuries the Church in Jerusalem and other parts of Palestine remained close to Judaism. Jewish believers in the Christ message were thought of as merely dissatisfied Jews. They followed many of the regulations of Judaism, such as abstaining from eating blood, pork and other prohibited foods. Also, they observed many Jewish feasts, ceremonies and traditions, some of which are still observed by the members of the ancient churches in the Near East.

At this early stage, however, what we call "Christianity" was a new movement within the bosom of Judaism and it did not concern the Gentile world. The fifteen first bishops of Jerusalem were all

Semites. Gentiles were not elected to high office until the third century, when the Roman Empire recognized Christianity as the state religion. At that time the emperor exercised great influence in electing church officials.

What happened to these early Jewish followers of Jesus? The answer is that they were assimilated by the Syrian (Aramean) and other Christians of the Semitic race. Jewish converts were a small minority when compared to the followers of Jesus in Syria and Mesopotamia. One must also realize that Jewish followers and all adherents to the gospel were expelled from Judea and many of them were martyred.[5]

Part 2—SPEAKING IN TONGUES. It seems that during that time, Semites were gifted in learning other languages very easily. As a general rule, shepherds, fishermen, farmers and even unlettered people were able to speak two, three or four languages, including several dialects. In the Near East, a dialect is often considered as a distinct language, not so much because of fundamental differences in words, but because of the differences in idioms and pronunciation. The reason for these differences was the lack of printing and of general communications between the tribes. In some regions, even a few miles distance between two towns creates a distinct difference in pronunciation.

Some learned men speak as many as twelve or more dialects as well as several languages. Because biblical lands have been conquered and ruled by other races, to learn a dialect or a foreign language is one of the highest aspirations of young men. And since one language is used at court, another for commercial transactions and still another for social relations, this ability has a very real, practical value.

Semites are clannish and strongly dominated by their respective religions, traditions and customs, so much so that intermarriage and social activities between members of rival faiths are discouraged. Each racial group clings to its own tongue and cultural background.

---

[5] See Acts 8:1.

However, even today one can still find three or four languages spoken in a town or city.

The people who were gathered for the feast of Pentecost were Galilean residents of Jerusalem and other Galileans as well as members of the Ten Tribes and foreign Jews who had come to the feast. The ancestors of the Galileans had been brought from various parts of the Near and Middle East and settled in Galilee by Assyrian kings in the eight century BCE. They spoke several Aramaic dialects and had preserved the customs of the countries from which they came.

Also present were Hebrew followers of Jesus' gospel of the kingdom. They were members of the ancient Ten Tribes and had been converted by Jesus and the seventy disciples he sent out to the "lost sheep of Israel," some of whom were settled only a few days journey from Galilee. Additionally, among the people who were visiting Jerusalem during this feast were Syrians from Tyre and Sidon, all of whom had close racial ties and spoke various Aramaic dialects and other tongues.

The disciples were inspired by the Holy Spirit. Some of them had traveled in Mesopotamia and Asia Minor. Quite naturally, the multitude, unused to such a spectacle, found it difficult to comprehend what had taken place. They thought that the apostles were drunk. The Holy Spirit had empowered them to speak so that they could be understood by all those who were willing to accept the truth of Jesus' gospel of the kingdom.

Part 3—GALILEAN DISCIPLES. With the exception of Judas of Iscariot, all of Jesus' disciples were Galileans.[6] Jesus began preaching and teaching in Galilee and was himself a Galilean. Most of the three years of his preaching was spent in towns around the lake of Galilee and in Syria. Jesus made several journeys into Judea but he was not well received there. Although he made some converts to his

---

[6]See Errico and Lamsa, *Aramaic Light on the Gospel of Matthew,* "Galilee of the Gentiles," pp. 50-52, and *Aramaic Light on the Gospel of Mark and Luke,* "Exposed by Speech," pp. 84-86.

gospel and had some sympathizers in Jerusalem and other towns, many Judean Jews—especially the scribes, Pharisees and upper class—rejected him. It was difficult for them to accept a Galilean prophet. They said that the Messiah/Christ must be born in Bethlehem of Judea.[7] "Out of Galilee ariseth no prophet."[8]

Since the days of the first captivity, Galilee had been known as the land of the Gentiles. When the king of Assyria removed the Ten Tribes from northern Israel, he settled in their place Assyrians, Chaldeans (Babylonians) and people of other races that were brought from the other side of the river Euphrates.[9] Isaiah called the inhabitants of this region "Gentiles," meaning foreigners.[10]

THE APOSTLES MAKE THEIR STAND

Others mocking said, These men are full of new wine. But Peter, standing up with the eleven, lifted up his voice and said unto them, Ye men of Judea and all ye that dwell at Jerusalem, be this known unto you, and hearken to my words For these are not drunken, as ye suppose, seeing it is but the third hour of the day. Acts 2:13-15.

Part 1—NOT DRUNK WITH NEW WINE. The Aramaic text reads *meritha*, "the dregs of new wine." *Meritha* settles to the bottom of the jar when wine is purified. Generally, these dregs are given away to the poor and strangers for them to drink, but the pure wine is kept in containers or earthen jars to mellow.

The disciples were not drunk with the dregs of new wine; they were filled with the Holy Spirit and inspired with confidence in their master and his teaching. Jesus' resurrection and his victory over death were confirmed by the new miracles of healing that the apostles themselves were able to perform and by the election of a new disciple

---

[7]Jn. 7:41-42.
[8]Jn. 7:52.
[9]2 Ki. 17:23-24.
[10]Isa. 9:1-2.

who filled Judas' place. Their hearts were fired with fervent zeal. They were ready to teach the gospel of their lord everywhere, regardless of difficulties and hazards that they were to meet. The truth had opened their eyes so they understood things spiritually. Up until this time, they had been students who had only understood things partially; now they could comprehend the meaning of the prophets and the inner secrets of their Jewish faith.

This change was so sudden that it was very difficult for the common people to grasp the situation. They knew that the disciples were simple Galilean fishermen and peasants. They were amazed to see these men conversing with Jews, Galileans, Syrians, Assyrians, and members of the Ten Tribes who had come to the Passover from every part of the world. As they could not understand the real cause of this unusual change, they thought these men might have drunk the dregs of new wine. Then again, in the Near East it is often said that "he is drunk," meaning "he is overcome."

These disciples were inspired by the Holy Spirit that gave them the power to speak, teach and preach. Jesus had promised them that the Spirit would teach them and guide them in all matters.

Part 2—APOSTLES TESTIFYING. The other eleven apostles stood up with Peter to prove that they were not drunk, as the people supposed, and to show that they were of one mind and one accord.

During banquets and festivals a speaker may stand or sit as he addresses his audience. It depends on the size of the group and the place. Peter stood up so that the people might see him; the crowd was very large. We are told that 3,000 of them were converted and baptized. There were others who did not believe and who rejected Peter's message.

Peter did not announce his subject at the outset. In the Near East, good preachers and speakers first try to prepare the minds of the people and acquaint them with what they intend to say. That is, the subject of the sermon and the most debatable portions of the talk are left for the end of the speech. This is done to avoid quarrels and disruptions of the meetings, which often happens on such occasions.

If Peter had begun by preaching his ideas about the messianic claims of Jesus, his resurrection and ascension, many Jews who were gathered there and who were not converts or sympathizers would have been offended and would have walked out. Some of these men would have started a riot, because to them these words would have sounded like blasphemy. Therefore, Peter began his speech with Jewish history, quoting from the prophets and offering evidence that Jesus of Nazareth, whom the Jews had rejected, was the very promised Messiah/Christ who was foretold by the Hebrew prophets.

In the middle of his talk, Peter announced his theme: "Jesus of Nazareth, a man approved of God among you by miracles and wonders and signs, which God did by him in the midst of you, as ye yourselves also know."[11] The apostle, concludes with: "Therefore let all the house of Israel know assuredly, that God hath made that same Jesus whom ye have crucified, both Lord and Christ."[12] Many of the Jews who were present had seen Jesus and witnessed some of his miracles and wonders. Peter's words recalled these things to their minds, so they began to think about Jesus, the things that he had done and the peaceful way in which he went to the cross. They were won.

Stephen also preached in the same manner. He announced the subject of his speech toward the end.[13] He begins with Abraham and gives an outline of Jewish biblical history in an attempt to prove that Jesus was the Messiah.[14] But some Jews were not moved by his plea, so they stoned him as a blasphemer.

The apostle Paul also used this style in his letters and during his trials in Jerusalem and in Caesarea. But on some occasions, as soon as Paul made known his subject, a riot ensued that led to his stoning or arrest.

Part 3—THE THIRD HOUR. It was probably about three in the afternoon. In the ancient Near East, time was reckoned on the basis of sunset to sunset. A new day began at sunset, 6 p.m., and morning

---

[11] Acts 2:22, K. J. V.
[12] Acts 2:36, K.J.V.
[13] See Acts 7:56.
[14] Acts 7:1.

broke at 6 a.m.

In certain areas where clocks were (and still are) unknown, time was measured by the falling shadows and by the sunbeams coming through the chimney in the center of the roof, and by crowing roosters. Some Semites can tell time by instinct. Shepherds rely on the stars during the night, and during the day they reckon time by the shadows of the trees and cliffs. Where there are no cliffs or trees, time is measured by a man's own shadow.

Peter did not consult a timepiece to convince the crowd that he was not intoxicated when he said, "It is but the third hour of the day." What he meant was that it was too early to indulge in drinking. In the Near East, wine is drunk only at meals, and as Semites seldom eat breakfast, wine is never used in the morning.

The disciples were inspired with a new zeal and enthusiasm. They were drunk with the feeling that their new faith would quickly become successful. Near Easterners frequently make remarks about someone being "drunk with wealth" or "drunk with power," meaning that the individual is over zealous or too extreme in his emotions.

People were amazed to see these unlearned disciples preaching and expounding spiritual matters and interpreting what to the priests was a mystery. These disciples had earlier thought and reasoned materially; now they saw everything from a fresh spiritual point of view. It was no wonder that it made a great stir and that outsiders were at a loss to account for these strange and unusual happenings.

UNIVERSE MOURNS

And I will shew wonders in heaven above, and signs in the earth beneath; blood and fire, and vapour of smoke; The sun shall be turned into darkness, and the moon into blood, before that great and notable day of the Lord come. Acts. 2:19-20.

This quote is from a prophecy by the prophet Joel.[15] Darkness,

---

[15] See Joel 2:28-32.

in this instance, refers to "mourning, disaster and calamity." The term "blood" means "death and destruction." The ancients believed that nature shared in man's joys and tragedies.

Even to this day, these terms of speech are very prevalent in Semitic languages. When kings, princes, or men of nobility die, professional mourners, in their songs of lamentation, portray the sun and the moon refusing to shine light because they are participating in the tragedy. Semitic people do not take these terms literally. They know they are written to reveal the magnitude of the calamity.

Peter referred to Joel's prophecy because he believed that the outpouring of the Holy Spirit was the beginning of the last days and that God was beginning to dismantle the political and religious systems of this world. This would be done by the coming of the Spirit, empowering Jesus' disciples to demonstrate God's kingdom on earth.[16]

JESUS CHOSEN BY GOD

Him, being delivered by the determinate counsel and foreknowledge of God, ye have taken, and by wicked hands have crucified and slain: Whom God hath raised up, having loosed the pains of death: because it was not possible that he should be holden of it. Acts 2:23-24.

Part 1—PREDESTINED. The Aramaic text, verse 23, reads: "The very one who was chosen for this purpose from the very beginning of knowledge and will of God, you have delivered into the hands of wicked men, and you have crucified and murdered him."[17]

Peter's charge against Jewish religious authorities is very strong. He explained that Jesus, although he died the death of a criminal, was not a sinner, as his accusers had thought him to be, but that he was chosen by God for this purpose from the very beginning of the

---

[16]See Jn. 16:8 and Errico and Lamsa, *Aramaic Light on the Gospel of John,* "Holy Spirit Rebuking World," pp. 191-192.

[17]Acts 2:23, Aramaic Peshitta text, Lamsa translation.

knowledge and will of God. According to Scripture, God created man in his image and likeness. Figuratively speaking, God knew that the human family would depart from grace and that nothing but the truth for which Jesus had died would restore humanity to its original self, the image of the creator.

Through Jesus' death, God's abundant and infinite love for the entire human race would be revealed; therefore, his death on the cross was inevitable. From time immemorial, God had sent prophets to preach justice so that humanity could come to the truth, but many of these prophets were denounced and rejected and others were slain. God knew that Jesus also would meet the same fate.

Jesus, on many occasions, predicted his rejection and suffering. He told his disciples that he would be crucified. He expounded upon all the Scriptures, beginning with Moses and the prophets, to prove to them that the Messiah/Christ was destined to die on the cross.[18] Also, according to Luke, angels told the women: ". . . Remember how he spoke unto you when he was yet in Galilee, saying, The Son of Man must be delivered into the hands of sinful men, and be crucified and the third day rise again."[19]

Jesus was chosen from the very beginning to be the Deliverer of the human family. The Jewish authorities and religious leaders, in rejecting him, played an important part in this great drama. Their act brought salvation and blessings to all humankind. Jesus cried from the cross: "Father, forgive them for they know not what they do." Jesus did not hold this wrong against them. They ignorantly crucified God's messenger of truth and salvation. The role they played was inevitable and the outcome would be victorious because God had raised Jesus from death.

Part 2—GOD RAISED JESUS. The Aramaic text, verse 24, reads: "Whom God raised up, having destroyed the pains of death, because it was not possible for *Sheol* to hold him."[20] According to the

---

[18] See Lk. 24:26-27.
[19] Lk. 24:6-7, K. J. V.
[20] Acts 2:24, Aramaic Peshitta text, Lamsa translation.

Jewish belief of the time, *sheol* was a powerful place from which no one had ever been able to escape. But Jesus, through his resurrection, destroyed the power of sin, death and *sheol*. The pain of death is fear and separation, but the risen Christ gave life a new synthesis and religion a new meaning.

Death was painful to those who did not know that God has power over it and *sheol*. For death holds no fear for those who live in the realm of the spirit and believe that God is the only power in the universe. When we understand death as a function of nature and life eternal, death and the grave lose their power.

ACCORDING TO THE FLESH

Men and brethren, Let me freely speak unto you of the patriarch David, that he is both dead and buried, and his sepulchre is with us unto this day. Therefore being a prophet, and knowing that God had sworn with an oath to him, that of the fruit of his loins according to the flesh, he would raise up Christ to sit on his throne. Acts 2:29-30.

The phrase "according to the flesh" refers to anything "carnal, earthly and terrestrial." According to the prophecy, Jesus, in his humanity, was supposed to be a descendant of King David.[21]

But one must realize that the promise to David was also a spiritual promise. The term "seed" in Aramaic also means "teaching." For example, Abraham is called the father of all believers and yet not all of his descendants were heirs of the promise. Only those who believed in the faith of Abraham were known as the children of Abraham.

King David was a symbol of the highest loyalty to God. Though he sinned and committed many crimes, David always repented and turned to God. Jesus' loyalty to God was even greater.

These promises are spiritual, for David's dynastic line ceased in 586 BCE when Jerusalem was destroyed by the Chaldean army. Since

---

[21]Psalm 132:11.

that time there has never been a blood heir of David to sit on his throne. The promise could only be fulfilled spiritually. Also, the expression "son of David" was commonly used among the people and it meant "like David." In the Near East, a great warrior is often called the son of another great and famous ancient warrior. This is the greatest honor that can be bestowed upon a leader or fighter.

King David lived a thousand years before Jesus. The Messiah was expected to be a great conqueror like David; he was to deliver the Jews from their oppression. The Messiah/Christ, the Spirit, is the son of God and existed even before Abraham.

Luke tells us that the angel Gabriel told Mary that her son would be called "Son of the Highest." (Note the use of the future tense in this verse. "He *will be great*, and he *will be called* the Son of the Highest, and the Lord will give him the throne of his father David."[22]) However, Luke does not trace Jesus' lineage through the royal line of the kings of Judah. He traces him through Nathan, another son of David, but not the crown prince. Jesus as the Christ was greater than David. For even David, in the spirit of prophecy, had called the coming Messiah "Lord."[23]

BREAKING BREAD

And they continued steadfastly in the apostles' doctrine and fellowship, and in breaking of bread, and in prayers. Acts 2:42.

In the Near East, bread is broken by hand before it is eaten. Table knives and forks were unknown. Customarily it is considered a sin to cut bread with a knife.

Bread is baked thin and round. A loaf is about seven inches in diameter. Before people begin to eat, a prayer is said by a religious man, if one happens to be present, or by an elderly person. Generally,

---

[22]Lk. 1:32.

[23]For a further explanation, see Errico and Lamsa, *Aramaic Light on the Gospel of Matthew*, "The Terms Son of David and Lord," pp. 277-279.

before breaking bread, Christian Semites make the sign of the cross on the forehead and say "in the name of God."

At times when bread is scarce, loaves are broken and divided evenly among those sitting at the table. When a religious man or a high official is present, people wait until he begins eating.[24]

The apostles and their followers met on the first day of the week for prayer and religious instruction. They ate bread together as a token of fellowship and as a memorial of their master. The apostles composed certain prayers that were recited before the group started to eat. This was done because the early followers of Jesus at that time did not know how to pray. An ancient liturgy called the Liturgy of the Apostles was compiled in the first century and is still used by the ancient Church of the East.

Bread was brought by the people who came for instruction. Paul admonished some of the members of the congregation to eat their meals in their homes and to eat and drink less during the meetings. Some men came just to eat and drink.

This ancient custom is still observed by Assyrian Christians. Baskets of fresh baked bread and food are distributed by one or several elderly women, who stand at the rear of the church or at the entrance. This is because some of the men and women travel long distances to attend the service. It is also true that whenever Semites visit each other, they always break bread together.

The breaking of bread and participation in eating together was the beginning of the communion service. Also, the Jews ate food offered at the temple, especially on Passover Day when every Jew participated in the eating of unleavened bread and lamb.

COMMUNAL LIFE

And all that believed were together, and had all things common; Acts 2:44.

---

[24] 1 Sam. 9:13.

Near Easterners are noted for their generosity and hospitality. They share food and clothing and shelter strangers and the needy. Members of the same faith call one another "brother" and stand by each other in time of danger and need.

"In common" should not be confused with communism. Jesus, in his teaching, never introduced communistic notions as we know them today. He warned his followers against the mammon (wealth) of this world and required those who became his disciples and followers to divest themselves of their earthly possessions. In those days the possessions usually consisted of sheep and cattle. However, Jesus encouraged his disciples and followers to be generous.

In this case, "in common" means everyone was generous and ready to help, even to the extent of selling their sheep and fields. It was done willingly and without being forced or made obligatory. Even in the Near East today, sheep, money, lands and lives are sacrificed for the sake of religion when necessary. By no means were the disciples encouraging every convert to sell his field or sheep. This would have created extreme poverty and idleness among the early followers. There were situations, however, when women and men who had no children turned their property over to the apostles, as in the case of Ananias and his wife Sapphira.[25]

We do not know how many of the new followers did this. But we know that such acts were done voluntarily. Paul, in his epistles, solicited funds from Christians in Asia Minor and Macedonia for the relief of the members in Jerusalem. In his letters, he admonishes congregational members to give according to their ability. He does not ask them to sell their cattle or fields. "So let every man give according to what he has decided in his mind: not grudgingly, or of necessity: for God loves a cheerful giver."[26]

In those days, the early followers of the Christ movement considered one another as brothers and as family. They were persecuted, hated and looked upon as a peculiar people. They had to

---

[25] Acts 5:1.
[26] 2 Cor. 9:7, Aramaic Peshitta text, Lamsa translation.

stand by one another and support those who were in need. Charity is one of the highest examples of Christian life. How can one say that he loves his brother when he sees him hungry and naked, but passes him by?[27]

BREAD—HOSPITALITY

And they, continuing daily with one accord in the temple, and breaking bread from house to house, did eat their meat with gladness and singleness of heart. Acts 2:46.

Part 1—EASTERN CUSTOM. Semites, when visiting one another's homes, eat bread together. A neighbor or a stranger who enters the house while members of the household are eating is invited to sit and eat with them. One who enters after or before the meal is asked if he has eaten or would like to eat. Most of the guests and visitors eat when they are asked. Some decline, however, expecting to be urged by the host a number of times. A host will usually beg the guest at least seven times to sit down and partake of the meal.

When priests and prominent men enter a house, the women immediately begin to cook and set the table for them. When Jesus entered the house of Martha and Mary, Martha started cooking and making preparations.[28] This hospitality is shown as a token of honor. Whether the visitor is hungry or not, he must eat something, for the family's feelings would be hurt if he refused. The only time an Easterner refuses to eat in the homes of others is when he has bad intentions against them. Once they break bread together, they refrain from doing any harm to each other.

This passage should not be interpreted as referring to the breaking of bread in Church.[29] When the disciples visited the homes of other believers, they ate bread with them, not because they were

---

[27] James 2:14-20.
[28] Lk. 10:39-41.
[29] Acts 2:42.

hungry, but because it was the custom. During feasts a person may visit ten to fifteen homes within a couple of hours and must eat something in all of them.

The term "bread" in Aramaic means "food." When a host asks a guest if he has eaten, he says, "Have you eaten bread?" This means, "Have you had your lunch or supper?" When a family is impoverished, it is said of them that "they have no bread." The reason for this is that in the Near East bread is the main article of food and no meal is complete without it. People consume a large quantity of bread at each meal.

These early followers of Jesus were glad to prepare meals for the apostles. The latter had no homes but were maintained by the generous and pious men and women who thought that the sharing of their food with the apostles would receive God's blessing.

Part 2—THE TEMPLE. Jesus' disciples and followers prayed in the Jewish temple and in the synagogues for many years. Their master had told them that he had not come to destroy the Torah but to fulfill it. Jesus did not start a new religion based on teachings alien to the Jewish prophets and holy Scripture. He simply attempted to restore the true teachings of the prophets that had been supplanted by the traditions of the elders and conflicting commentaries.

For years the Jews permitted the followers of Jesus to worship in the temple. For a time they did not suspect them of being leaders of a new movement that was growing very rapidly. These early followers of Jesus' gospel of the kingdom kept the Sabbath, circumcised, abstained from the worship of images and the eating of blood. They also celebrated the Jewish feasts. Indeed, for the time being, they were identified with the Jewish faith.

CHAPTER 3

LAME HEALED

Then Peter said, Silver and gold have I none; but such as I have give I thee: in the name of Jesus Christ of Nazareth rise up and walk. Acts 3:6.

Customarily, Semites give food, lodging and clothing to the poor and to beggars. Money is so scarce that few men would think of handing over a silver or gold coin to a beggar. Until the 1940s, only a few people carried money on them when at home. Gold coins were so scarce that in many places people had only heard of them but had never seen them. Those who did possess gold and silver usually buried it in the ground or carried it in a small *tarmala* (bag) or in their sash. Copper coins were more plentiful and were freely carried about and at times given to beggars.

Begging is commonly done on street corners or at holy places, where tourists and strangers are likely to be present as well as women and men who have taken vows and have come to pray. Such people are good prospects, for they will probably have some silver or gold with them and because vows and sincere prayers tend to make one feel more benevolent. An expert beggar, therefore, would not waste time on townspeople who knew him and saw him every day but would keep an eye out for pilgrims, whom he could easily recognize by their attire. He always hopes that some wealthy person with plenty of gold or silver might be generous enough to toss him a few coins.

Peter and John had come from Galilee. They were strangers in Jerusalem. The lame beggar at the gate did not expect bread or clothing from them, but he supposed that they must have some money for the purchase of food, lodging and other necessities. So he urgently begged them for help, expecting a silver or gold coin. Peter said: "Just take a look at us." He wanted the beggar to notice that they were almost as poor as he. "We have no silver or gold to give you; but we do have the power to heal which is far better. In the name of Jesus of Nazareth, stand up and walk."

Hearing their words, the beggar believed and immediately stood up and walked; then, with much leaping and rejoicing, he walked into the temple to give thanks. The genuineness of his ailment is attested by this act, for had he not been really lame, he would have cursed Peter and John for not giving him money. Also he would certainly not have wasted his time going into the temple when he could be begging by the gate. He wouldn't want to miss the opportunity of finding a wealthy donor.

The apostles gave him something that money cannot buy. His faith in Peter and John had healed him and the sincere words uttered by Peter opened his eyes to see a new world where sickness, sin and poverty are unknown. The secret is this: when one believes in those who have power and an inner understanding of God, one receives health, happiness and prosperity. "Believe his prophets and you will be delivered."[1]

FAITH IN HIS NAME

And his name through faith in his name hath made this man strong, whom ye see and know; yea, the faith which is by him hath given him this perfect soundness in the presence of you all. Acts 3:16.

The Aramaic text reads: "Faith in his name has healed this man, whom you see and know, and made him strong; it is the faith in him which has granted this healing before you all."[2]

The expression in this verse "faith in his name" means faith in Jesus' teaching—that is, Jesus' way or method of approach to God. Jesus taught his disciples to pray and look to God as a loving father, the beloved. He also taught them to love their enemies as he did.

"Faith in his name" also refers to believing that Jesus is the promised Messiah/Christ, who was sent by God. The apostles used

---

[1] 2 Chron. 20:20, Aramaic Peshitta text, Lamsa tranlation
[2] Acts 3:16, Aramaic Peshitta text, Lamsa translation.

the same method of healing that they had learned from their master. They did what they had seen him do.

PETER WITNESSES TO THE CROWD

Repent, ye therefore, and be converted, that your sins may be blotted out, when the times of refreshing shall come from the presence of the Lord; And he shall send Jesus Christ, which before was preached unto you. Whom the heaven must receive until the times of restitution of all things, which God hath spoken by the mouth of all his holy prophets since the world began. Acts 3:19-21.

Part 1—REPENTANCE. "Repent" in Aramaic means "to turn to God." By turning to God—that is, to truth and light—one's sins are blotted out. Peter admonishes the crowd to turn to God and be converted to Jesus' gospel of the kingdom.

Those whose sins are blotted out become relieved of the heavy burdens they were carrying and find, thereafter, a state of harmony and tranquillity. This is what it means by "the time of refreshing shall come from the presence of the Lord." Once people have repented and their hearts are cleansed, then the Christ, God's truth, becomes a living part of them.

As long as evil forces and inclinations dominate a person's heart and mind, truth cannot come, for truth and error cannot dwell together. Even as fire and water are contrary to one another, truth and error, evil and good, cannot be placed in the same vessel. When truth comes in, error is destroyed.

Part 2—MESSIANIC PROPHECIES. The Aramaic text, verse 21, reads: "Whom heaven must receive until all the things which God has spoken by the mouth of his holy prophets since the world began should be fulfilled."[3] This verse refers to the messianic prophecies. The Aramaic world *molaya* means "fulfillment." The prophets had predicted the coming of the Messiah/Christ, his suffering, death and

---

[3]Acts 3:21, Aramaic Peshitta text, Lamsa translation.

resurrection. And these divine prophecies had to be fulfilled. The death of Jesus was a way of salvation that the prophets had foreseen. Jesus surrendered his life knowing that through his death and resurrection, he destroyed the fear of death.[4]

Isaiah had predicted that the Messiah was to suffer. Moses also foretold of the coming prophet like himself.[5] Other prophets from Samuel to John the Baptist had testified concerning the coming of the Messiah.

Peter's tone is meek. He tries to prove to the Jews that these things had been prophesied and therefore had to come to pass. He further says that those who had rejected Jesus as the Christ still had an opportunity to repent. Peter does not condemn the Jews for the death of Jesus, but he urges them to repent and receive the blessings that God has prepared for them.

According to Peter's message, Jesus would remain in heaven until everything concerning the final triumph of the gospel of God's kingdom is fulfilled. The prophecies that foretold his coming and crucifixion had already happened, he declared, but those of his final return are to be fulfilled in the fullness of time—that is, when the reign of God is established permanently on earth.

The Jews expected a sudden restoration of the kingdom of Israel, to be followed by the eternal presence of the Messiah, who would conquer and rule forever. But Jesus told his disciples that the kingdom was not to come suddenly but in the process of time. It would come slowly, like the working of leaven that takes considerable time to ferment the dough.

The Messiah/Christ has already come and his kingdom is among us, but it will be a long time before the whole world will see the true meaning of his teaching and commands. As the races of this world gradually become true disciples in their hearts and minds and adhere to Jesus' teaching, then his return is hastened. People will feel the Christ presence everywhere. They will see him just as those who

---

[4]2 Tim. 1:10
[5]Dt. 18:15.

believed in him saw him after his resurrection. He will guide them as he guided his original disciples and followers. He assured them that he would not leave them alone but would remain with them until the end of the world. Thus the Christ is here today for those who know him and believe in him. His spirit has been a guiding influence from one generation to another; his words are light and life to those who receive them.

CHAPTER 4

BUILDERS

This is the stone which was set at nought of you builders, which is become the head of the corner. Acts 4:11.

This quotation is from Psalm 118:22. Jesus, while debating with a certain group of Jews, made reference to this passage: "The stone which the builders rejected, the same is become the head of the corner."[1] The Aramaic text reads "the cornerstone."

In the Near East a man who wants a new house must furnish stones, beams and other material necessary for construction. The contractor is at liberty to reject certain stones and beams if he should find them too hard to hew or simply not suitable for the house. Generally, this is done because large stones, which must be lifted by hand, are hard to place in the wall. However, when stones are too big for the wall, they may be used as cornerstones. Smaller stones are placed over them and defects are hidden. At times, the builder and the owner of the house may argue as to whether large stones should be rejected. Peter called this stone a "rock of offense" because the builders were offended.[2]

Jesus was rejected as Messiah/Christ on the grounds that he was a Galilean and not of the lineage of David. The Jews insisted that when the Messiah comes he will be born in Bethlehem and will be a descendant of David. "Others said, This is the Christ. But some said, Shall Christ come out of Galilee? Hath not the scripture said, That Christ cometh of the seed of David, and out of the town of Bethlehem, where David was?"[3]

The Jewish priests and elders—the builders—found it difficult

---

[1] Mt. 21:42, K. J. V.
[2] See 1 Peter 2:8, K. J. V.
[3] Jn. 7:41-42, K. J. V.

to accept Jesus' teachings; therefore, they rejected him and his message of God's kingdom. Thus he became the cornerstone upon whom a larger movement was to be built. Paul called Jesus the "chief cornerstone," which is the largest stone in the building.[4]

Jesus as the Messiah/Christ is the stone that the builders rejected but has become the cornerstone of the spiritual movement that became known as "Christianity." Jesus is the image and likeness of God. He demonstrated what it is to be a genuine, spiritual/human being and was a model of justice, peace and love for all humanity.

UNLEARNED AND IGNORANT

Now when they saw the boldness of Peter and John, and perceived that they were unlearned and ignorant men, they marvelled: and they took knowledge of them, that they had been with Jesus. Acts 4:13.

All the disciples of Jesus, with the exception of Matthew, were illiterate and uneducated. Most of them were fishermen from the small towns around the lake of Galilee. Up until the turn of the 19th century, Near Eastern fishermen, farmers and shepherds seldom acquired an education. They believed it was a waste of time. These men were assigned in their youth to occupations that they were to carry out when they grew older. When they were young they worked with older men as helpers and assistants in farming, fishing and tending sheep and cattle. Only boys who were destined to be employed in government service or to become ministers of religion were educated.

Matthew was educated to become an employee of the government. In his career as a collector of taxes and customs duties, he succeeded to the office of chief publican, a high position in Eastern countries.[5] The other disciples were instructed in their own homes and later by Jesus. He taught them how to teach, answer questions

---

[4]Eph. 2:20-21.
[5]Lk. 19:2.

and how to conduct themselves during feasts and banquets as representatives of his new gospel of the kingdom.

Jesus' disciples spent three years with him and heard him debating with the priests and lawyers (scribes), talking to and helping and healing individuals with mental and emotional problems, preaching in the synagogues, and teaching large and small groups outdoors. They observed how he handled himself in difficult and challenging situations. They remembered many of his answers when questioned by the scribes and Pharisees. When the disciples were confronted with such questions themselves, they replied with similar answers.

This is why the high priests and the council were astonished when they heard these illiterate men preaching, debating and quoting Scripture. They realized that these men had been with Jesus. In that part of the world in those days and up until the 1800s, education and knowledge were largely transmitted by word of mouth. Some of the most learned and capable men in the Near East cannot read or write, but they know the law and are good speakers and advisers. The same is also true even with some wise men and kings.

The apostles' minds were free from complicated teachings and traditions of men. They were taught by Jesus and inspired by the Holy Spirit. Their faith in Jesus and his teaching enabled them to meet every situation and solve any problem. But the council, feeling that the disciples were ignorant and misled, let them go, hoping they would stop preaching and return to their old occupations.

THINGS IN COMMON

And the multitude of them that believed were of one heart and one soul: neither said any of them, that ought of the things which he possessed was his own; but they had all things common. Acts 4:32.

Isolated religious communities are still to be found in many parts of the Near East, especially in Mesopotamia, Syria, and the Arabian desert. People of peculiar beliefs and strange customs prefer to live with others of their own faith and as far away as possible from their enemies and people of other faiths. They know that their religious teachings and some of their odd customs are resented by members of other religions who predominate in large towns and cities.

Such a religious community or sect is usually governed by a hereditary chief who exercises both spiritual and temporal authority over them. In many instances, he is the patriarch, judge, lawmaker and treasurer of the tribe. These people are strongly united by sacred tribal bonds and by means of marriage among their own kin. They are always ready to help, or even to fight and die for one another. This unity is necessary for the safety, survival and welfare of the community or tribe that is surrounded by natural enemies and by members of rival faiths.

In some cases, food and money are entrusted to the chief of the tribe. He also cares for surplus supplies of food and clothing and, in time of need, he distributes them among his people. Members of the community often wear one another's clothes and shoes. They also borrow oxen for plowing, and, at times, they do this without asking permission. For example, the Sabians in Iraq, who are known as the people of St. John, live very close to each other and never associate or eat with others. To some extent this is true of another group known as Devil Worshipers, who live in northern Mesopotamia. They also live a communal life, working in the interests of one another. There are also Jewish and Assyrian communities in Turkey whose racial ties are very strong and who share and help each other. One can never find them in want or begging.

The early followers of Jesus were living a similar life style as the above mentioned communities. The situation that they were facing called for a communal life. Money and material things were given and taken freely. These people considered themselves as one family.

The Aramaic text reads: "Now the congregation of believers were of one soul and of one mind; not one of them spoke of the property he possessed as his own; but everything they had was in common."[6] "Everything they had was in common" must not be understood literally. It does not mean that everything they had was put together. There were several thousand followers in the holy city and such a radical way of living would have aroused suspicion among the Jews and Roman authorities. Cities are not logical places for commune living. What happened was this: The apostles had designated certain places in the inns as places for the poor. These places were supported by certain believers who had businesses or thriving occupations. Again, food and clothing were distributed among those who had shelter but were poverty stricken.

Fields were sold because people wanted to leave the city and because they feared persecution and that their property would be confiscated. The new movement was outlawed from the very beginning; its teachings were declared contrary to both the Jewish and Roman institutions. These authorities, at the outset, did not take cognizance of the importance of the movement, but when they saw its steady growth, they took steps immediately. The believers were expelled from Palestine and some of them murdered. Some of the early followers sold their fields and homes at this time. Perhaps it was only those who had no children or other responsibilities, so they could live with their brethren. But, at any rate, they did it of their own accord.[7]

A true religion and spiritual teaching abolishes racial and geographical barriers. The teachings of Jesus were to unite all races with a sacred bond. Faithful believers in the Christ are members of the same family. Through Jesus' kingdom message they realize that they are children of God. This spiritual bond, peace and understanding are more important than money, fields and other material things.

BARNABAS

And Joses, who by the apostles was surnamed Barnabas (which is,

---

[6]Acts 4:32, Aramaic Peshitta text, Lamsa translation.
[7]Acts 5:4.

being interpreted, The son of consolation), a Levite and of the country of Cyprus, Having land, sold it, and brought the money, and laid it at the apostles' feet. Acts 4:36-37.

Part 1—THE SON OF CONSOLATION. Barnabas was a Jewish convert from Cyprus. He had a field and sold it, bringing the money to the apostles to dispose of as they saw fit. Barnabas was selected by the Holy Spirit to work with Paul among the Gentiles.[8] He went with Paul to Cyprus where they preached in Jewish synagogues.

Paul and Barnabas were working among Jewish communities that were scattered throughout Syria, Asia Minor, Greece and other parts of the Roman Empire. Most of these people were descendants of the Ten Northern Tribes of Israel that had been exiled from Palestine by the Assyrians. During the Persian conquest of Asia Minor and Greece many of them settled in these regions. Other Jews from Palestine were also scattered throughout the civilized world at that time.

Jesus had instructed his disciples to go first only to the descendants of the Ten Tribes. These people were friendly to Paul and Barnabas and helped them in their work. But the Palestinian Jews, who often invited them to speak in their synagogues, eventually turned against them because they quickly discovered that the apostles were teaching ideas contrary to the established faith.

Barnabas was a missionary among the Jews, but little is known about him outside of his travels with Paul. It seems that there were some differences of opinion between him and Paul over the Gentile question. This was probably the reason he eventually left Paul. Nonetheless, Barnabas went with Paul to present the case of the Gentiles before the apostles[9] and then went with Paul to Antioch.[10] He was an early follower of Jesus' gospel of the kingdom and a Jewish disciple of the Christ, who, like Paul, labored faithfully in the interests of the new movement.

---

[8] Acts 13:2-4.
[9] Acts 15:2.
[10] Acts 15:22.

Part 2—AT THE FEET. Placing money "at the feet of the disciples" does not mean that it was literally put at their feet, but that is was given to them to do with as they pleased—that is, at their disposal. "At their feet" is an Aramaic idiom that means "given without any strings." The idiom also means "in their care" or "at their mercy." The particular interpretation of the idiom is determined by the context. Semites often say that "he threw himself at the governor's feet," meaning he placed himself under the governor's care or service. "I put my house and all my wealth at your feet" means that the house and wealth are yours to do anything you please with them.

In the Near East, people often turn over all their property to certain religious teachers or institutions and are then supported by them. Some of them live and work with priests, bishops and other holy men of distinction. They devote most of their time to prayer and other religious activities connected with the sanctuary, such as cooking, waiting on tables and other household work. They are supported by the offerings brought by the people to shrines and religious leaders. Thus, it is common even today among Assyrians, Kurds and Arabs to find men and women who have left or sold their properties and are living in the household of religious teachers.

However, cases like this were rare among the early followers. Only a few men among them ever sold their fields. This was not a model for a communistic economic pattern. Neither Jesus nor his apostles ever contemplated or entertained such a notion. But some of the followers turned their wealth over to the apostles and went preaching the gospel of the kingdom. Usually, their property consisted of sheep and cattle, just as it does for some people today. Of course it would be necessary to relieve themselves of these responsibilities so that they could be free to travel and preach.

Apparently, incidents similar to those of Ananias and Shapphira[11] occurred only in Jerusalem and a few other places in Palestine where opposition to the new teaching had forced them to unite and stand by one another. There were no such examples in Asia

---

[11]See Acts 5:1-10.

Minor, Macedonia or other countries. Paul appealed to Christians in Asia Minor and Greece to give contributions to the elders in Jerusalem, but he never asked them to sell all of their property and become paupers. Jesus taught his followers to practice liberality, but he put no premium on poverty as an expression of piety.

Barnabas was called by the Holy Spirit to become a companion to Paul and to preach the gospel of the Christ. He sold his field and turned the money over to the apostles to be used for the cause of the gospel. Jesus' joyful message had opened his eyes and given him a new understanding of life. Therefore, Barnabas had pledged his life to God. And so it was easy for him to donate the price of his field for the sake of God's kingdom. Sincere and pious men and women in the Near East give everything for the cause of their faith and are ready to die for it. As far as they are concerned, they are "laying up treasures in heaven" and not "treasures buried in the ground."[12]

---

[12] See Mt. 6:19-20.

CHAPTER 5

MEN OF GOD FEARED

And Ananias hearing these words fell down, and gave up the ghost: and great fear came on all them that heard these things. Acts 5:5.

The Aramaic text reads: "But a certain man called Ananias, together with his wife named Shapphira, sold his field. And he took some of the money and hid it, and his wife also knew of it, and he brought some of the money and placed it at the disposal of the apostles. And Simon Peter said to him: Ananias, why has Satan so filled your heart that you should lie to the Holy Spirit and hide part of the money of the price of the field? Was it not your own before you sold it? And after it was sold, had you not the sole authority over its money? What made you think to do this thing? You have not only lied to men but to God. And when Ananias heard these words, he fell down and died; and great fear came upon all of those who heard these things."[1]

People in ancient biblical lands fear and revere religious men, especially those who are recognized as genuine men of God. They seek blessings and healing from these holy men. But, people also are afraid of curses or rebukes uttered by such men. For, just as the people believe that a holy man possesses certain powers by which to heal the sick and restore the insane, they also believe this holy man has power to put a curse on anyone.[2] In the Near East, when persons charged with crimes are brought before a man of God, they fear his power and tremble before him. Criminals who successfully defend themselves during their trials in court confess their crimes and plead guilty when they are brought in the presence of a holy man.

Ananias and his wife had sold their field. They were probably

---

[1] Acts 5:1-5, Aramaic Peshitta text, Lamsa translation.
[2] As a matter of fact, Dr. Lamsa saw some men guilty of crimes become stricken suddenly after being cursed by a religious man.

too old to take care of their land. They wanted to turn over a portion of the money to the apostles and keep some for themselves for emergencies. They had decided to join a group of pious believers and live with them. Of course, the field was theirs, and no one had forced them to sell it. After it was sold, the money was also theirs and no one could have taken it away from them. Therefore, there was no reason to lie about the money that they had received for the price of the field.

What upset and disturbed Peter was that they lied about the sale and not that they had withheld a portion of the money. They were not obligated to give all of the money they had gained from the sale of their property. Zachaeus gave only half of his wealth when he embraced the gospel that Jesus had preached to him.[3]

What happened was this: As Peter looked into their faces and asked them about the price of the field, their expressions changed and their eyes betrayed them. The lie was apparent to Peter; he sensed something was wrong. He suspected that they were not honest about the sale price and could not be trusted. Such corrupt people who would lie and cheat when they didn't have to say or do such things did not belong with the family of believers in God's household.

Both Ananias and his wife were stricken not by God but by their own guilt and dishonest hearts. Realizing that they had deliberately lied to the principal holy man, Peter, and in the midst of the presence of God (the Holy Spirit) and the people, they died. Just as truth gives courage and life, lies generate fear and death.

HEALING POWER

There came also a multitude out of the cities round about unto Jerusalem, bringing sick folks, and them which were vexed with unclean spirits: and they were healed every one. Acts 5:16.

---

[3] Lk. 19:8.

From the very beginning of their ministries, the apostles tried to follow in the footsteps of their master. They preached the gospel of the kingdom of God, taught, baptized and healed the sick as Jesus had commissioned them to do. The first case of healing at their hands created considerable interest among the people and helped to confirm their faith. Both believers and unbelievers saw that the disciples were endowed with powers similar to those of their master.

The lame man they had healed was a witness to this hidden power, possessed by no one besides Jesus and his disciples since the days of the prophets.[4] Naturally, the news about their healing power would spread faster than that of their preaching because the people who were healed were eager to spread the word of God and help the healers.

"Unclean spirits" in Aramaic refers to the mentally and emotionally ill. Prior to the development of medical science, the causes of insanity were unknown. At that time, mental illness was attributed to demons and devils (jinn). Even today in certain areas of the Near East, bishops and healers often rebuke "unclean spirits" and some of these ill people are restored in this manner. The principle is this: Good destroys evil and truth corrects error. Faith in Jesus as the Messiah/Christ restores souls and brings healing to the mentally and physically ill.

APOSTLES IMPRISONED, ESCAPE AND TEACH

But the angel of the Lord by night opened the prison doors, and brought them forth and said, Go, stand and speak in the temple to the people all the words of this life. And when they heard that, they entered into the temple early in the morning, and taught. But the high priest came, and they that were with him, and called the council together, and all the senate of the children of Israel, and sent to the prison to have them brought.
Acts 5:19-21.

---

[4] Acts 3:6.

Part 1—AN ANGEL OPENS THE DOOR. The term "angel," *malakha* in Aramaic, means "God's messenger, a pious man, an ambassador, an innocent man, a minister." In the Near East, miraculous acts are generally attributed to higher powers. Heavenly beings are called angels and are seen in dreams and visions. They appear at night or while an individual is in a trance.

Angels are spirits. They have no physical bodies, but in a dream they appear like men and converse like human beings. They appeared to Mary, Joseph, Gideon, Daniel and to many other holy men and women.

The apostles were helped by God. The door was opened in a mysterious, miraculous way. According to Semitic belief, God intervened and helped the apostles escape through a secret messenger sent by God. "The host of angels of the Lord encamps round about them that worship him, and delivers them."[5]

Part 2—TEMPLE GROUNDS. The temple in Jerusalem was divided into several parts—the inner and outer courts,[6] the holy of holies, the place of worship and the treasury (where women stood during prayer). The outer court was used by the Gentiles, who were not permitted to enter the holy grounds.[7] The temple compound was enclosed by a stone wall.

The apostles, like their master, preached to the people whom they found gathered at the court of the Gentiles, the outer court. The Jews did not permit unbelievers to enter the temple proper. They would not permit even their own if they were not consecrated properly to address the people. The high priest was the only person who, once a year, entered the holy of holies, presenting an offering for the sins of the people. The temple pattern, rituals and procedure were very similar to those of the ancient tabernacle that Moses erected in the desert.

The place where the people gathered for prayer and religious

---

[5]Ps. 34:7, Aramaic Peshitta text, Lamsa translation.
[6]1 Ki. 7:12; Ezek. 8:16.
[7]Rev. 11:1-2.

discussions was something like a common, such as Boston Common, or Hyde Park in London. Anyone can address the people on such grounds, but certainly not from the pulpits of great cathedrals or churches.

In the Near East, temple grounds are used for public meetings. One often sees people gathered at the church courtyard, debating, discussing town affairs, and resting. Others pray standing close to the church wall. Such grounds, at times, prove very useful for a stranger who wishes to contact the people and preach to them.

DOCTORS

Then stood there up one in the council, a Pharisee, name Gamaliel, a doctor of the law, had in reputation among all the people, and commanded to put the apostles forth a little space; Acts 5:34.

The Aramaic word for "doctor of religion" is *malpana*, meaning "teacher." This was the term used by the Jews when they referred to learned men. At that time, the usual studies were limited to the five books of Moses (the Torah), and the prophets. In most cases, the title *malpana* was given by the people to an outstanding teacher. Generally, the title that people bestowed upon an excellent preacher was *rabbi* meaning "my great one." Jesus was called *malpana tawa*, meaning "skilled and wonderful teacher."[8]

The learned scribes also were called *malpaneh,* "teachers." Some of these men were copyists; others had made a deep study of Scripture and therefore were recognized as "doctors." Some of them taught in the temple and sat in the councils. "And it came to pass that after three days, they found him in the temple sitting in the midst of the doctors, both hearing them, and asking them questions."[9]

The Romans had taken from the Jews most of their political and

---

[8] See Mt. 19:16 and Errico and Lamsa, *Aramaic Light on the Gospel of Matthew,* "Wonderful teacher," pp. 242-243.

[9] Lk. 2:46. See also Mk. 12:28-34; 1 Tim. 1:7.

economic freedoms, but they allowed them complete jurisdiction in religious and social affairs. The Mosaic law was still the law of the land. Matters of property division, marriage, divorce, and all religious affairs were handled by learned Jews. Scribes and teachers of the Torah rendered decisions in all such cases. These scribes represented the Jews in Roman courts and pleaded the cause of the Jewish faith before the Roman governors and other officials, as was the case in the trials of Jesus and Paul.

BEATEN

And to him they agreed: and when they had called the apostles, and beaten them, they commanded that they should not speak in the name of Jesus, and let them go. Acts 5:40.

In the Near East, when people are rebuked for minor religious or civil offenses, those in charge of punishment will either strike the offenders on their cheeks or beat them on their backs. Soldiers or servants administer the beating. However, when people commit major offenses, they are punished more severely. A guilty person is stripped of his clothing and laid on the ground, face down. Then, two men stand one on each side of the offender and begin beating him with straps or sticks until his back is black and blue and bleeding from the severe punishment.

The apostles may have been lightly punished by a few slaps on their cheeks or more severely punished with straps. Whatever the punishment was, they took it with joy. They had done no wrong. They remembered what their master had told them, that they would be thrown into prison and beaten for the sake of his gospel of the kingdom.[10]

Followers of the Christ teaching must be willing to pick up their crosses—meet the challenges, whatever they may be—under all conditions. Punishment and imprisonment should not be permitted to

---

[10]Mt. 10:17.

hamper the preaching of the gospel of the kingdom. Throughout the history of the Christian movement, martyrs have served as the highest examples of devotion to Jesus and his teaching. Their suffering and death strengthened the faith of the believers, brought others into the fold of Christianity, and helped to spread the gospel. All those who have preached the truth and stood for justice and true piety have suffered in one way or another.

CHAPTER 6

HELLENISTIC JEWS

And in those days, when the number of the disciples was multiplied, there arose a murmuring of the Grecians against the Hebrews, because their widows were neglected in the daily ministration. Acts 6:1.

The term "Grecians" in this verse means "Hellenists"—that is, Jews who were unorthodox, having been Westernized under Roman rule. The Revised Standard Version more correctly reads: "Grecian Jews." The Lamsa translation of the Aramaic text reads: "Hellenized converts."

Some of them may have been Jews who had returned to Palestine from Greece, Egypt, Alexandria and Cyprus just as today American, Polish, Italian, Russian and German Jews are returning to Israel. In some areas they are still known by the name of the country from which they come. At that time, these followers of Jesus were Jews by race, but their practices and customs were more Gentile than Palestinian, Jewish manners.

In those days, all Jews who did not live strictly by the Mosaic law and its ordinances were called "Greeks, foreigners." At the turn of the 1900s in Turkey, all Muslims who drank liquor and ate forbidden foods were called either *aleman, fransai or agnabi,* "German, French, or foreigner." Also, Near Easterners are often identified by the name of the party or sect to which they belong. Many years ago, for instance, members of a Young Turkish Party were called *aleman,* "Germans," because they were pro-German. Other Turks were known as "French or English" for the same reason. Armenians who have joined the Presbyterian and Congregational churches are referred to as "Americans." Syrians who are members of the Greek church are called "Greeks." The Assyrians who belong to the Roman Catholic Church are known as "French."

At this early time, the Galilean movement was restricted to the people of the Jewish religion and to members of the Ten Tribes of Israel. For centuries, these people had been expecting the coming of the Messiah, the great deliverer. On the other hand, Greeks knew nothing about messianic promises nor had they heard of the Hebrew prophets and patriarchs. During this period in history, Greeks, like the Romans, were aliens and enemies of the Jews.

Discrimination against members of rival faiths is characteristic of Semites. Members of the same race who belong to various sects complain against and mistrust one another, especially in the case of relief. Missionaries and relief workers find this to be as true today as it was in the time of the apostles. The reason for this is that leaders of every sect or group are eager to help their own people, and members of one sect mistrust the leaders of the others, no matter how honest they may be. Even today, the members of some religions and sects complain, charging that there is discrimination against their people.

Evidently some of the early Jewish orthodox followers of Jesus' teaching discriminated against the Hellenized, Jewish believers in Jesus. In the Near East, when such issues arise, headmen from every race and faith or sect are selected to look after each group. Racial customs and traditions have always been a barrier between the various members of the Christian denominations and, at times, have split the church into many factions. This entire matter is a departure from the teaching of Jesus, who taught unity and equality. Believers in Jesus' teaching from all races and customs are united in a sacred bond. In Christ there is neither Jew nor Gentile.[1]

One of the men whom the apostles chose to administer food, supplies, and other help for widows was Stephen, a Jew.[2] A great many Jews used Greek and Roman names, as today they use English, German, Italian and Russian names. When Stephen began his address to the Jews with the calling of Abraham in Acts 7:1-2, he addressed the Jews as "men, brethren," that is, members of the same Jewish faith and race. This shows that Stephen was Jewish although he had

---

[1] Gal. 3:28.
[2] See Acts 6: 2-5.

a Greek name.

Today, Arab Christians in Palestine who are members of the Greek Orthodox Church call themselves "Greeks" although they are not Greeks by blood. They do this so that they can be distinguished from Christian Arabs who call themselves Roman Catholics and from others who call themselves Monophysites or Maronites. The apostles had to resolve these issues that were arising and challenging the progress of the movement.

STEPHEN

And the saying pleased the whole multitude: and they chose Stephen, a man full of faith and of the Holy Ghost, and Philip, and Prochorus, and Nicanor, and Timon, and Parmenas, and Nicolas a proselyte of Antioch: Whom they set before the apostles: and when they had prayed, they laid their hands on them. And the word of God increased; and the number of the disciples multiplied in Jerusalem greatly; and a great company of the priests were obedient to the faith. And Stephen, full of faith and power, did great wonders and miracles among the people. Then there arose certain of the synagogue, which is called the synagogue of the Libertines and Cyrenians, and Alexandrians, and of them of Cilicia and of Asia, disputing with Stephen. Acts 6:5-9.

Part 1—STEPHEN STONED TO DEATH. Stephen was a Jew who, like many other Jews, had become a faithful follower of Jesus and believer in the gospel of the kingdom. At this early time, nearly all of Jesus' disciples and followers were members of the Jewish religion. Jesus had come first to the Jews. A transformation of religion was to take place and the seeds of the gospel were to be sown first in Jewish soil. This is because Jesus was following in the footsteps of the Hebrew prophets who had hailed the coming of the Messiah. Jesus had come to fulfill the law and the prophets.

Stephen had assumed a Greek name. This was a common practice, especially among those Jews who did not adhere strictly to the Jewish law and traditions of the elders. These men adopted foreign names wherever they lived.

Stephen was martyred by stoning. Had he been a Greek, the Jews could not have stoned him. The charge against him would have been referred to the Roman authorities, who had sole jurisdiction over all people not of the Jewish race. The Jews had authority to stone only those of the Jewish faith who were accused and tried by their council and convicted of blasphemy or other violations of Jewish law and its ordinances. This authority was restricted to the province of Judea. No Gentile Roman citizen could have been put to death for blasphemy against the Mosaic law. The Jewish council tried and convicted Jesus, but because he was a Galilean they could not enforce the death penalty called for by their law.[3] So they delivered him to the Roman governor who, as a representative of the emperor, had authority over all people in Palestine. Jesus was crucified by Gentile soldiers.

The charges against Stephen were these: "... we have heard him say blasphemous words against Moses and against God."[4] Stephen was a strict and learned Jewish man. This is the reason the priests and scribes were alarmed at his utterances, which they construed as blasphemy. In his wonderful defense before the council, he gave the Jewish leaders a concise outline of Hebrew history, their forefathers and their messianic hopes.[5]

Part 2—LAYING ON OF HANDS. The practice of the laying on of hands indicates approval, appointment and consecration. The hand is also symbolic of divine power. When Near Easterners select a lamb to be sacrificed at a shrine, they lay hands on it, indicating that it has been given to God. When a girl is engaged, people say "they have put hands on her," meaning that she is pledged to marry. Jewish priests and leaders were consecrated by the laying on of hands. "And the Lord said unto Moses, take thee Joshua, the son of Nun, a man in whom is the spirit, and lay thine hand upon him."[6] The people also

---

[3] Jn. 19:7.
[4] Acts 6:11.
[5] See Acts 7.
[6] Num. 27:18.

laid their hands on animals that they sacrificed for the sin offering. "And Aaron shall lay both his hands upon the head of the live goat . . .And the goat shall bear upon him all their iniquities. . . ."[7]

By laying on of hands, Semites believe the Holy Spirit is imparted from one person to another. Therefore, all consecrations for such ministry are done by the bishops and other higher authorities by the laying on of hands. Jesus laid his hands on his disciples when he sent them to preach the gospel, and they, in turn, laid hands on the believers after they were baptized, thus confirming them in the faith that Jesus taught. This ancient Hebrew custom was practiced by the apostles and their followers and is still practiced by many Christian churches throughout the world.

The seven deacons selected were ordained to help the apostles in the administration of relief and other minor duties. They acted as assistants to the apostles, teachers and preachers. The office of the deacon in Aramaic is called *meshamshana,* "minister." The *kahna,* "priest," prefers not to celebrate communion without one or two deacons.

Part 3—CONVERTS. "Priests" mentioned in verse seven is a mistranslation. The Aramaic text does not make a reference to the "priests." It reads: ". . . And many people of the Jewish faith became converts." There is no evidence that a single Jewish priest was converted at this particular time. Priests, scribes and many Pharisees had been hostile to the new teaching from the very beginning. Most of the early followers were recruited from the illiterate and lower classes. "Then answered them the Pharisees, Are ye all deceived? Have any of the rulers or of the Pharisees believed on him? But this people who knoweth not the law are cursed."[8]

Priests and learned men usually have been the last to change their beliefs. As religious leaders, they generally depend on the teachings and traditions of their faith whether these be right or wrong. Truths are more readily revealed to simple men and women whose

---

[7]Lev. 16:21-22.
[8]Jn. 7:47-49.

minds, like those of little children, are free from complicated theories and theologies. This is why Jesus told his followers to become like little children so that they may enter (participate in) the kingdom of God.

BLASPHEMY

Then they suborned men, which said, We have heard him speak blasphemous words against Moses, and against God. Acts 6:11.

According to Jewish law, blasphemy against God and the holy temple was a criminal offense and the person thus convicted was to be stoned. "And thou shalt speak unto the children of Israel, saying, Whosoever curseth his God shall bear his sin."[9]

When King Ahab was unable to purchase Naboth's vineyard, he sought two false witnesses who said that they had heard Naboth blaspheme God and the king. Then they took him out and stoned him.[10] It was against the law to revile God or the ruler of the people.[11]

The accusations against Jesus were similar to those made against Stephen. At the outset, he was charged with blaspheming "the temple of God."[12] The charge against Stephen was that he had blasphemed God, the Torah and the temple. The false witnesses testified that they had heard him say that Jesus of Nazareth would destroy the temple and change the law and the customs of the people.[13]

Stephen was a Jew who had become a faithful believer in Jesus and in his gospel of the kingdom. The Jewish council in Jerusalem had the power to put him to death if they found him guilty of violating the Jewish laws. The Romans had granted the Jews some authority in religious matters. Had the charge against Stephen been

---

[9] Lev. 24:15, K. J. V.
[10] 1 Ki. 21:13.
[11] Ex. 22:28.
[12] See Mt. 26:60-62.
[13] Acts 6:13-14.

political, they would have accused him before the Roman governor, as was the case concerning Jesus of Nazareth and his trial. But the charge was a religious one. Roman authorities were unfamiliar with Mosaic law and its ordinances. On the other hand, like the British and French, they were careful and preferred not to interfere with the laws and customs of the land, especially the religious laws and ordinances.

The Mosaic law and Jewish customs were respected and kept by the Jewish believers and many followers of Jesus who were of other Semitic races. Jesus had told his disciples that he had not come to destroy the law but to fulfill it. Therefore, it is obvious that Stephen did not actually blaspheme against the Torah. He was misunderstood just as Jesus was misunderstood when he spoke about the kingdom of God.

CHAPTER 7

STEPHEN'S MESSAGE

And he said, Men, brethren, and fathers, hearken; The God of glory appeared unto our father Abraham, when he was in Mesopotamia, before he dwelt in Charran. And said unto him, Get thee out of thy country, and from thy kindred, and come into the land which I shall shew thee.
Acts 7:2-3.

Part 1—ANCIENT MESOPOTAMIA. "Mesopotamia" is the Greek term used for Iraq. During the time of Abraham, however, the land was called Beth Naharain, "the house between the rivers." Mesopotamia in Greek also means "between the rivers." The rivers referred to are the Tigris on the east and the Euphrates on the west. Iraq is almost like an island between these two historic rivers. The land was also called Assyria and Chaldea. Ur of the Chaldees is near Babylon in the southern part of Mesopotamia. This is the place from which Abraham migrated to Palestine.[1]

Haran now is called Hauran. The King James Version of this verse calls it "Charran." The region is northeast of Galilee close to the border of Syria. In Aramaic the name of the place is Aram-Padan. Abraham and the people who were with him dwelt there for many years; from there he journeyed into Palestine. But some of his kindred did not follow him; they chose to remain in Haran. Abraham was a Chaldean, but his early descendants were know as Arameans. Later these people were called "Hebrews," which means "the people who crossed the river."

In his last days, Abraham made his servant promise to go to Haran to his relatives and bring a wife for his son Isaac. He did not want Isaac to marry outside of his own kinsmen.[2] Jacob also, when he fled from Esau, went to Haran to the home of his uncle Laban. He

---

[1] Gen. 11:31.
[2] Gen. 24:1-4.

remained with his uncle 21 years and married two of Laban's daughters and later their maids. He returned with considerable wealth to Palestine.[3]

Stephen in his address gave a very brief summary of the Hebrew history, their migrations and struggles that led to the messianic promises and the old covenant. He was attempting to prove to them that Jesus, whom their fathers had rejected, was the very Messiah who had been predicted by the Hebrew prophets. He was claiming that Abraham had been called by God to leave his land and people and go to Palestine for this very purpose.

Part 2—TRIBAL MIGRATION. Tribal migration has always been very common in Arabia, Syria and Western Persia. Chiefs and elders of the tribes meet together to discuss tribal affairs, with water supply, pasturage, migration and tribal security being among the major topics of concern. Nomadic people are constantly on the move. They cannot stay at one place. Usually, they are looking to find new pastures. The sustaining of their flocks and herds is dependent on so many changing conditions. When the wells become exhausted and dried out, a move is inevitable.

Migration from cities and inhabited regions is not caused by population growth. It is due to the rapid increase of flocks and cattle that usually takes place during periods of peace. Semites live chiefly on milk, cheese, butter and other associated products. So sheep and cattle are seldom killed for food. They are the tribe's most valuable possessions. The increase is amazing; for example, a family with twenty five sheep may, in a decade, become very rich, possessing flocks of several hundred.

Owing to the increase of flocks and the consequent scarcity of pasture lands and water, brothers often divide their sheep and cattle, one remaining in town in charge of land and other immovable family possessions, while the other brother leaves the country in search of better grazing lands and greater prosperity.

Such migrations are very slow and difficult. It might take almost

---

[3]Gen. 29:1-28.

a decade for a migrating tribe to reach its chosen destination. It is challenging to meet the needs of a large company of people made up of several brothers and their families, a retinue of servants and numerous flocks and herds. The task is especially difficult with pastures to find, wells to be dug and wars to be fought with contesting tribes along the way. And the birth of young calves and lambs naturally makes traveling anything but speedy. Occasionally, tribes settle and remain in a favorable location for a considerable period of time, some of them even building houses and planting crops, and living like peasants rather than nomads.

Terah, the father of Abraham, required many years to travel from Ur in Chaldea to Haran in Syria. He had brought with him many of his kinsmen with their servants and flocks. They marched westward, halting in some places several years on their way to Haran. Their destination seemed to be Palestine, but the migration was interrupted by Terah's death. Years later Abraham took Lot, his nephew, with his family and servants and resumed the journey to the promised land.

In biblical towns this country was known as the kingdom of Soba and its people were called Arameans. Damascus was the capital. It was conquered by David, but afterward the people revolted and became the chief adversary of Israel. This kingdom was one of those overthrown during the Assyrian conquest of Syria and Northern Palestine in 722 BCE, when the Ten Tribes were taken away as captives to Assyria.

ANCIENT STUDIES

And Moses was learned in all the wisdom of the Egyptians, and was mighty in words and in deeds. Acts 7:22.

When scientific studies such as economics, medicine, engineering and navigation were in their infancy, magic was considered a science and an art. It was favored over other knowledge. In some countries magic was the principal subject of study and almost the only means of education. Many ancient manuscripts containing magic formulas and secrets have come down from the past. Some of these works still survive in Near Eastern countries and are still taught to students who desire to become magicians. Also, any person who is in possession of such rare documents of magic is looked upon as a magician and is often consulted by the people for advice and help.

When men lose some of their sheep or cattle on the mountains, they rush to a magician or a priest who is in possession of a book of magic and beg him to tie up the mouth of the wolf and bear so that they may not attack the lost animals. The magician takes a knife out of the sheath and prays and leaves it out until the animals are found. It is supposed that whenever the wild animals see the sheep, the mouths will not close and therefore they will not bite or harm them. When this act is performed by a religious man, through faith in the power of God and prayer, it usually works, and the lost animals are found safe.

Centuries ago even chemistry and astronomy were considered as magic. Moses had studied these things when he was in Egypt, not because he wanted to become a magician, but because these were the usual studies offered in those days. This is why he acted as a magician when he appeared before Pharaoh. His work surpassed that of the state magicians. He also studied Egyptian law, administration, religion and ethics. In ancient times, state laws and religious laws were one and the same.

Moses did not create two sets of laws, one for religion and another for the state. He wrote a single code that embodied both. Indeed, Moses was familiar with both Chaldean (Babylonian) and Egyptian laws and sciences.

REVERENCE TO GOD

Then said the Lord to him, Put off thy shoes from thy feet: for the place where thou standest is holy ground. Acts 7:33.

Where ancient customs are practiced, Semitic Christians always remove their shoes when they enter a church or a house. Muslims still do when they enter a Mosque. And, to sit down uninvited when in the presence of a ruler or a high government official is a breach of etiquette. But to enter a church, synagogue or mosque with shoes on is sacrilegious. It is not permitted at all. Near Easterners believe that in church they are standing in the presence of God.

Stephen retells the biblical episode when the God of Israel appeared to Moses in the burning bush. God told Moses to remove his shoes because the ground on which he stood was holy. Moses was born and reared in Egypt, and according to many legends, he was educated in the knowledge of all Egyptian sciences and religion. The book of Exodus actually does not tell us where or how Moses obtained his learning. Concerning his childhood and tutoring all we know is: "And the child grew, and she brought him to Pharaoh's daughter, and he became her son. And she called his name Moses; for she said, I drew him out of the water. And it came to pass in those days when Moses was grown up, that he went out among his brethren and saw the oppression. . . "[4]

According to traditional stories, when Moses was at the palace, he probably sat in the presence of Pharaoh, attended national ceremonies, and worshiped at the Egyptians' shrines and temples. Moses had seen men taking their shoes off and bowing before the priests and images in the shrines.

During the time of Abraham, the Hebrews were unaware of any such protocol, pomp or ceremony. They were a sheep-raising people, living a simple life in tents furnished with a few small blankets made of lamb's wool. These blankets were used for bedding, and a few large, flat stones served as chairs in their tents. There was no need to remove their shoes, nor do modern day people practice this in their tents.

When God appeared to Abraham and conversed with him, Abraham received him in a simple way, as another Arab chief would welcome a Semitic petty ruler. Abraham, in his vision, washed God's

---

[4]Ex. 2:10-11, Aramaic Peshitta text, Lamsa translation.

feet and set bread and buttermilk before him to eat.[5]

Reverence to God is man's highest expression of respect. God does not need or want the human family to bow and beg before his presence. But it is proper to revere God and enter places of worship with a clean heart and mind. "Removing one's shoes" is symbolic of the removal of earthly things from one's mind and a readiness to accept spiritual matters.

A GREATER PROPHET

This is that Moses, which said unto the children of Israel, A prophet shall the Lord your God raise up unto you of your brethren, like unto me; him shall ye hear. Acts 7:37.

The followers of Jesus believed this prophecy was fulfilled in Jesus of Nazareth, who was the greatest prophet since the days of Moses, and whose coming Moses had predicted.[6]

The phrase "of your brethren" is somewhat difficult to explain. Some authorities do not know why Moses did not say "from among you." Moses was addressing the Israelite people. The term "brethren" was often used to mean "people who are kindred of the Jews." For example, Abraham said to his nephew Lot, "We are brothers." The Edomites, the descendants of Esau, were also "brothers" of the Jews.

Other scholars suggest that the term "brethren," in this instance, refers to the "Galileans and the Arabs," who are kindred of the Jews. The Muslims maintain that this prophetic reference was to their prophet Mohammed, a descendant of Ishmael, son of Abraham.[7] However one may interpret this verse, Jesus is generally acclaimed as the greater prophet. He performed greater miracles and wonders than any who had proceeded him or who came after.

---

[5]Gen. 18:1-9.
[6]Dt. 18:15.
[7]Gen. 17:20.

THE TABERNACLE OF MALCOM

Yea, ye took up the tabernacle of Moloch, and the star of your god Remphan, figures which ye made to worship them: and I will carry you away beyond Babylon. Acts 7:43.

The Aramaic term *mashkna* (in Arabic *maskan*) means "tent, tabernacle," and it refers to the dwelling place of Malcom, the god of the Ammonites. This god, like the God of Israel, had a tabernacle in which he was worshiped by the tribal peoples, who migrated from one place to another carrying the tabernacle and the god with them. This temporal sanctuary was made of goat hair. Even today, the Emirs of Arabian nomadic tribes have such a sanctuary for worship and for assembly, which they carry with them wherever they go.

In the desert, the Israelites at Sinai carried the tabernacle of God from one place to another for a period of forty years, but when they departed from God, they carried the tabernacles of Malcom and other strange gods.

From time to time in Israel's history, the people turned away from Yahweh, their God, and were worshiping Malcom, the god of the Ammonites, thus carrying his tabernacle. They also were worshiping the different star gods. In this instance, they worshiped the star god, Derphan.

JOSHUA

Which also our father that came after brought in with Jesus into the possession of the Gentiles, whom God drave out before the face of our fathers, unto the days of David. Acts 7:45.

The Aramaic text reads: "And this very tabernacle, our fathers, together with Joshua, brought into the land which God took away from the peoples whom he drove out before them and gave it to them for an inheritance, and it was handed down until the days of David."[8]

In Aramaic, the Hebrew name "Joshua" is *Eshoa Barnun*, which means "Jesus, the son of Nun." Joshua led the twelve tribes of Israel into Palestine about 1400 BCE. Both the Hebrew "*Yashua*" and Aramaic name "*Eshoa*" mean "Yahweh saves or helps." Therefore, it may also be translated as "Savior."[9]

The tabernacle of the congregation, which was used as a place of worship in the desert, was brought into the holy land by Joshua. It was kept as a holy relic until the time of King Solomon.[10] Together with the ark and its sacred contents, it remained in Jerusalem until the city was taken and the temple burned by the Chaldean army in the year 586 BCE. From that time on, it simply disappeared.

The tabernacle was a large portable tent furnished with costly curtains and adorned with fine gold and precious stones. It was covered with sheep and goat skins. Whenever the people moved around in the desert, the tabernacle was dismantled and the ark of the covenant and its holy relics were carried by the priests and Levites.

The sheepskins and fabrics (made of the hair of goats) were probably worn out and became difficult to preserve long before the temple of Solomon was built. These materials could not have been kept for a period of four hundred years. The other parts that were made of gold, silver and shittim wood were undoubtedly preserved and later kept in the temple together with other sacred national relics. The Hebrews also preserved Aaron's staff, the tablets, a pot of manna and a few other holy objects, which were kept in the ark.[11]

DISPOSITION OF ANGELS

Who have received the law by the disposition of angels, and have not

---

[8] Acts 7:45, Aramaic Peshitta text, Lamsa translation.

[9] See Errico and Lamsa, *Aramaic Light on the Gospel of Matthew* "The Name Jesus," pp. 20-22.

[10] 2 Chron. 5:5-6.

[11] Dt. 10:5, 31:26.

kept it. Acts 7:53.

The Aramaic term *malakha* has several meanings. It can denote "angel, minister or messenger." The stem of the verb, not its root, is *mlkh;* it means to "counsel, advise." Angels are spiritual messengers that carry God's counsel and come to the aid of people who are open and receptive and who are in need of answers. Good and innocent people are also called angels. Jacob said to his brother Esau: "I saw you as an angel," meaning "I saw you innocent and harmless."

In the Middle Ages, angels were portrayed with wings, signifying God's omnipresence. In the book of Psalms, we read: "Who makest his angels spirits, his ministers a flaming fire."[12] "He made his angels spirit" means embracing all space—everywhere. God's counsel or guidance is everywhere and available to all those who are seeking to know the truth.

The law was given to Moses by God. Literally speaking, there was no intermediary between Moses and God. Moses spoke with God "face-to-face" and received the divine oracles directly from God. His revelation and communications were clear and plain.

During Stephen's time, sixteen centuries after the Torah was given to Moses, the people believed that God had become so holy and they had become so evil that God could not be approached directly by human beings. The only way to commune with God and to seek heavenly counsel was through mediators. This period was known as the deistic period. We see this in the priestly system of worship. The high priest had become the mediator between God and Israel. He entered the holy of holies once a year to pray for forgiveness and to intercede for the people.

The ten commandments were different from any other law in that they came directly from God's counsel, i.e., "the disposition of angels." Scripture tells us that the commandments were written by the "finger of God." This is a Semitic idiom and it means that the commandments were flawless and perfect.

---

[12] Ps. 104:4, K. J. V.

STEPHEN'S VISION AND DEATH

And said, Behold, I see the heavens opened, and the Son of Man standing on the right hand of God. Then they cried out with a loud voice, and stopped their ears, and ran upon him with one accord, and cast him out of the city, and stoned him: and the witnesses laid down their clothes at a young man's feet whose name was Saul. Acts 7:56-58.

Part 1—AT THE RIGHT HAND OF GOD. In Stephen's vision he saw Jesus "standing at the right hand of God." This is an Aramaic idiom that means "to have the authority and power of God."[13] Among the Semitic kings, the position on the right of the ruler is given to the queen or other high state dignitaries. During state ceremonies and other functions, the queen sits on the right hand of the king. When the queen is not present, the most important official of the government occupies this place of honor.

In Near Eastern countries, where kings and emperors were worshiped as deities, ministers of state always stand when in the presence of the monarch. In those days monarchs were inaccessible to their people; not even their wives could come into their presence without being called.[14] The Jewish concept of a ruling God was similar to their Eastern Semitic conception of a great monarch.

According to the Jewish theocratic idea of deity, no one could come close to God or see his face. For a man to stand at the right hand of God was a blasphemy or a contradiction of the Mosaic law. God was so holy that he could not be approached by mortals.[15] Not even great prophets like Moses and Elijah could see his face.

Jesus, in the eyes of Jewish authorities and priests, died the death of a criminal. Stephen's declaration that he saw the Son of Man (i.e., Jesus, a human being and believed to be a malefactor) standing at the right hand of God was a blasphemy according to Jewish understand-

---

[13]Compare Mt. 26:64. See also Errico & Lamsa, *Aramaic Light on the Gospel of Matthew,* "Before the Council," pp. 339-340.
[14]See Esther 4:11.
[15]Ex. 19:21-24.

ing of God.

It is likely that Stephen quoted the words of Jesus that we find in Matthew 26:64 and Luke 22:69. Such an assertion was intended to prove that Jesus was the promised Messiah/Christ and that the Jewish religious authorities were wrong in rejecting him. However, the Jewish officials believed that the Messiah was yet to come and that when he came he would be invested with great powers. They had repudiated Jesus' claims to this high office, and Stephen's address, therefore, only served to provoke and enrage them.

Part 2—GUARDING GARMENTS. "The witnesses laid down their clothes at a young man's feet" is an Aramaic idiom that means "in his charge or care." The young man to whom the garments were entrusted agreed to guard them until their owners returned. The clothes were placed on the ground beside him.

In the Near East, when men do hard work or any sort of physical exercise, they remove their flowing outer garments to avoid soiling them and to allow free movement of their limbs. The garments are taken off and placed in separate piles at a distance in the care of boys who keep an eye on them so that they will not be stolen or exchanged. As clothes and shoes are made by hand, they are scarce and their owners are afraid of losing them. Even during the hour of prayer, the worshipers are anxious about their shoes that are left outside the church or mosque. It often happens that men with worn-out shoes cut their prayers short and leave very quickly so that they can pick up a better pair for themselves.

During the hour of prayer, many Muslims bring their little sons to watch their shoes while they are praying. Some mosques have shoe-guardians whose job is to see that every person gets his own shoes returned after prayer. They look at each person and his shoes as he enters the mosque. They are trained to remember the faces of the worshipers and their particular shoes.

Paul, at this time, was too young to throw stones and participate in the murder of Stephen. But he performed his duty by guarding the garments of the men who were about to stone Stephen. Thus, he showed his zeal and devotion to the Jewish religion by taking care of the clothes while others did the stoning. This allowed him to participate without actually throwing any stones.

When a stoning takes place, those in charge take the man to a vacant place outside the city. Then the blasphemer is placed in the midst of the crowd and immediately the men encircling him commence pelting him with stones from a short distance. The stones are thrown from all sides so rapidly that the man is almost buried under them.

Another reason for laying aside their clothing is that, at times, the victim tries to escape from those inflicting the punishment. In attempting to stop him they may get their garments stained with his blood. Semites would consider themselves defiled if stained with the blood of a person who has been condemned for blasphemy.[16]

---

[16] Acts 8:1; 22:20.

CHAPTER 8

EVIL SPIRITS

For unclean spirits, crying with loud voice, came out of many that were possessed with them: and many taken with palsies, and that were lame, were healed. Acts 8:7.

The Aramaic text reads: "Many who were mentally afflicted cried with loud voices and were restored; and others who were paralytic and lame were healed." "Unclean spirits" is an Aramaic term used to describe mentally ill people. The Aramaic word *akhidan-way* means "possessed with a mental affliction" or "possessed by an evil power."

In those ancient days medical terms and the causes of diseases were not known. Most illness, especially mental and emotional, was attributed to evil spirits. Philip healed sick men and women—that is, those who were mentally and emotionally ill and others who were paralytic or lame. It was these people who cried out and gave thanks and not any evil spirits. When the sick are healed they shout praises and thanks to God and to the healer.[1]

MAGIC

And when Simon saw that through laying on of the apostles' hands the Holy Ghost was given, he offered them money. Acts 8:18.

Near Easterners teach and learn magic just like other arts and crafts. Magic is handed down from father to son. The secrets of the trade are not disclosed without some remuneration. Magicians, fortunetellers and workers of witchcraft often exchange information

---

[1] Compare Mk. 1:34. See also Errico & Lamsa, *Aramaic Light on the Gospels of Mark and Luke,* "Casting Out Devils," pp. 15-17.

with one another. Magic secrets are bought and sold. New secrets and practices are disclosed to disciples or to strangers who wish to acquire the much coveted art of magic and sorcery.

Both noted and less prominent magicians are besought by apprentices. Students of magic often pay large sums of money to acquire the secrets and the confidence of the masters whose popularity and reputations are well known and established. These students consider that their money and time are well spent because the art of magic is quite popular in the East. Usually those who practice it are very prosperous.

Magic was used as a sort of entertainment at banquets, weddings and special occasions. Even some wise men were skilled in the art of magic. This is why Herod expected that Jesus would perform some signs when Pilate sent Jesus to him.

Kings and wealthy men know and make use of magicians, fortunetellers and astrologers. They treat them with respect and honor them very highly. These tellers of fortunes, readers of the stars and performers of magic enter freely into palaces and homes of noblemen to demonstrate their acts.[2] They are well received and well paid. They also ask favors for their friends from rulers, governors and other high officials.

Moses and Aaron had little trouble in gaining permission to appear before the Pharaoh because they acted as magicians. Had they not been recognized as noted magicians, they would have been drafted into the army of slave laborers and sent to make bricks like other Hebrews.

Simon the magician had heard of Peter and John performing miracles and wonders in Jesus' name. At that time, Jesus' fame had spread throughout Palestine and Syria, and the miracles and wonders that he had done were remembered by the people and especially by the magicians. These men thought that Jesus must have had certain magic secrets and written formulas. Many magicians were eager to learn these secrets. The Jews, on many occasions, asked Jesus to

---

[2] Acts 13:6-9.

show them a sign.

Simon was most eager to meet Peter so that he could obtain some information about Jesus' secrets. He thought that he would have no trouble in purchasing this power. He probably had acquired his own knowledge of magic through monetary means. It was natural for him to think that he could purchase more knowledge with the money he had earned from his own practice of magic.

Simon did not know that what Peter and John had could not be purchased with silver or gold but could only be acquired through faith in Jesus and his teaching. When he faced the disciples, he not only failed to obtain healing powers, but his own practices were exposed. Truth abolished the error and hypnotic powers that Simon possessed.[3]

VISIONS

And the angel of the Lord spake unto Philip, saying, Arise, and go toward the south unto the way that goeth down from Jerusalem unto Gaza, which is desert. Acts 8:26.

In countries where modern means of communication were unknown and illiteracy dominated, many people relied on dreams and visions for communicating with friends and relatives. The popular belief in divine communication by such means was so fixed and firm that most people would follow the instruction given to them in a vision without any hesitancy or doubt.

When Joseph was told in a dream to flee to Egypt, he obeyed the command immediately. The Magi were also warned in a dream not to return to Herod but to return to their country by another route. They too followed the guidance from the dream.[4] When God appeared in a dream to Abraham and told him to leave his land and

---

[3] See Acts 8:20-24.
[4] Mt. 2:12. See Errico and Lamsa, *Aramaic Light on the Gospel of Matthew*, "Dreams and Visions, Part A" pp. 16-17.

go to a country that he was going to show him, Abraham departed without question. There are many passages in Scripture where God spoke to his prophets through visions. At this time, God communed with Peter, Philip, Paul and other apostles, instructing and guiding them in their preaching and work. Many books in the Bible are based solely on visions that men of God saw.

God has always revealed things through visions and dreams to those who seek guidance. The epistle to the Hebrews reads that "God, who at sundry times and in divers manners spake in time past unto the fathers by the prophets."[5] Today, as in ancient days, God speaks through Jesus' gospel of the kingdom. He calls men and women and sends them to declare his word, directing and guiding them in their work.

Philip was guided by a messenger (angel) in a vision and told where to go. He obeyed the divine command without doubt or hesitation. It was natural for him to trust in his vision.

AN ETHIOPIAN EUNUCH

And he arose and went; and, behold a man of Ethiopia, an eunuch of great authority under Candace, queen of the Ethiopians, who had the charge of all her treasure, and had come to Jerusalem for to worship. Acts 8:27.

PART 1—EUNUCH. A eunuch is a slave attendant in an Eastern harem or in the household of a wealthy man or a high government official. The custom of making eunuchs is an ancient one.

A eunuch cannot marry; therefore, he is assigned to certain duties in a harem or household. Some rulers employ a great many eunuchs. Some of the eunuchs are so trustworthy that they are greatly honored by their masters and are elevated to high government positions. Others become important advisors and confidants on social and political matters. On the other hand, some eunuchs are badly

---

[5]Heb. 1:1, K. J. V.

treated and may even be murdered.

Queen Esther, before she was brought into the presence of Ahasuerus, King of Persia, was placed under the care of Hegal, the King's chamberlain who looked after the welfare of the women. Hegal was a chief eunuch in charge of harems.[6]

Prior to World War 1, the Turkish and Persian kings, who had large harems, kept many eunuchs. In the 1930s and 40s some of the Arabian rulers who maintained harems employed eunuchs as guardians of women and children.

Jesus, when discussing marriage and divorce, spoke of eunuchs. He said that there are several classes of eunuchs: those who are captured and made eunuchs by force, those who are born eunuchs, and those who willingly make themselves eunuchs for the sake of the kingdom of heaven; that is, they become celibates for the kingdom.[7]

Up until the 1940s, this custom was still practiced in a few isolated and primitive areas in Africa and Asia. The League of Nations appointed a committee to see that this custom was discontinued. At that time, the emperor of Ethiopia had done everything within his power to abolish this ancient practice of slavery and to reform his people.

PART 2—ETHIOPIAN JEWS. Numerous Ethiopians were believers in the Jewish God and adhered to the Jewish customs and manners and many of them had come to the Holy City for worship and instruction in the Jewish law. It is said that one of their great queens, the Queen of Sheba, came to see Solomon and later married him. Historians say that the Queen of Sheba abolished pagan worship and accepted the Hebrew religion. Many Ethiopian tribes had become Jewish proselytes before Christianity was introduced into Ethiopia in the first century. The prophet Jeremiah mentions an Ethiopian eunuch at the court of king Zedekiah, named *Ebed-melech*.[8]

There were also many Jews in Ethiopia who fled to Africa after

---

[6]Esther 2:8.
[7]See Mt. 19:12.
[8]Jer. 38:7

the fall of Jerusalem in the year 586 BCE. Even today there are about 300,000 Jews in Ethiopia. They probably were settled there after the conquest of Jerusalem by the Chaldeans in 586 BCE.

FOLLOWING THE CHARIOT

Then the Spirit said unto Philip, Go near, and join thyself to this chariot. Acts 8:29.

The Aramaic word *kap* means both "to join" and "to follow," but in this case, it more correctly reads "to follow." In Palestine, strangers would not attempt to sit in the chariot of a distinguished person without being formally invited. Even when they are invited they must decline at first.

In a caravan a great many people travel together. Social distinctions are dropped so that the travelers might mingle and converse in a friendly fashion. The caravan deliberately moves slowly so that the people who are traveling on foot can keep up with the chariots. It is the poor who travel on foot and follow close behind the noblemen, who ride on horses or sit in chariots. They listen to conversations, especially when the person traveling is a wise man or a government official.

Customarily, a person riding in a chariot is either a prominent man or an official. He is surrounded on all sides by his servants for protection and as a token of honor. When on a long journey Semites easily became acquainted with one another and acquired the confidence and friendship of prominent travelers. They usually engaged in friendly conversations. Religious and racial barriers were laid aside so that the long and tiresome journey might become more pleasant.

This eunuch, the minister of finance, was a Jew by faith but Ethiopian by nationality. He had come to worship at the temple in Jerusalem, which was the central, most sacred shrine to all Jewish followers throughout the world.

Semites came from great distances to offer sacrifices and pray together at holy places. Some people traveled more than a thousand miles. Today Muslims from the Phillippine Islands, India, China and other far-off countries go to Mecca to pray. The Jews from Europe and the United States travel to Jerusalem for prayer and to visit holy places. This is equally true of Christians, who travel from Russia, Poland and other parts of the world to worship at the holy sepulcher.

PRAYING ON A JOURNEY

And Philip ran thither to him, and heard him read the prophet Esaias, and said, Understandest thou what thou readest? And he said, How can I, except some man should guide me? And desired Philip that he would come up and sit with him. Acts 8:30-31.

In countries where prayer is a habit and adherence to religion a duty, most people are content with the mere recital of a few oral or written prayers. This is true of some of the unlearned members of ancient religions; they read the sacred writings but make no effort to understand their inner meaning. Most of the sacred books were written in classical languages that to some extent differ from the vernacular speech. Therefore, difficult words and phrases are explained by the priests and learned men. Usually, orthodox Jews pray in their ancient Aramaic and Hebrew tongues. The general populace, with the exception of religious leaders, does not understand the meaning of these prayers that the orthodox Jews recite.

In some countries the language of one race is adopted as the sacred tongue by another race. For instance, the religion of Islam originated in Arabia and the Quran was written in Arabic; hence Arabic became the sacred tongue of Muslims, Hindus, Persians, Turks, Egyptians, Chinese and many other races whose members have embraced the Islamic faith. Many of these people can read Arabic but cannot understand the meaning of what they read. Even priests and learned men cannot come to an agreement about the meaning of certain words, because the parables, allegories and idioms in one language cannot be transmitted into another tongue without loss of meaning.

Undoubtedly, this Ethiopian eunuch could read the sacred scroll in Hebrew or Aramaic, but he could not understand the passage of Scripture that he was reading. He spoke Amharic, a language akin to Hebrew and Aramaic, but he needed someone to explain to him the meaning of the prophecy. Philip was led by the Spirit to give him the inner meaning of the this scriptural passage. Philip was following the chariot, but when he began to converse with the eunuch, the latter invited him to ride with him. The friendly conversation led to the conversion and baptism of the Ethiopian minister of finance. Philip was led by God who opened the eyes of the eunuch to the faith that Jesus taught.

SUFFERING MESSIAH

In his humiliation his judgment was taken away; and who shall declare his generation? For his life is taken from the earth. Acts 8:33.

The Aramaic text reads: "In his humiliation he suffered imprisonment and judgment; none can tell his struggles. For even his life is taken from the earth."[9] The phrase that reads "none can tell his struggles" means "no one can fully relate the facts and hardships."

The Aramaic word *dara* means "struggle, conflict, trial, war." The letter *heh* "h" is added to the word to indicate possessive case, *dareh,* "his struggles." The letter *resh* "r" is doubled in pronunciation. Thus *dara* becomes *darra*. Aramaic speaking people and writers use the same word for "generation" or "a period of time," but they do not double the consonant "r." This is the reason translators were unable to see the difference. This word is rarely used to mean "war" or "generation." There are other Aramaic words for this which appear frequently in Aramaic literature.

---

[9] Aramaic Peshitta text, Lamsa translation.

This verse refers to the conflict that Jesus fought against opposing forces, his struggles, trial, judgment and suffering on the cross. These were predicted by the prophet Isaiah: "He was oppressed and he was afflicted, yet he opened not his mouth: he is brought as a lamb to the slaughter, and as a sheep before her shearers is dumb, so he openeth not his mouth."[10]

During his trial, Jesus hardly said anything. He refused to reply to the accusations that were brought against him. He bore his cross and prayed for his enemies. Jesus entrusted his soul to God, his Father, with the assurance of triumph and ultimate victory.

CAUGHT AWAY BY THE SPIRIT

And when they were come up out of the water, the Spirit of the Lord caught away Philip, that the eunuch saw him no more: and he went on his way rejoicing. But Philip was found at Azotus: and passing through he preached in all the cities, till he came to Caesarea. Acts 8:39-40.

In Aramaic the phrase "the Spirit of the Lord caught away Philip" has several meanings. In a dream or vision, it can mean to be lifted by the spirit from one place and taken to another. This happened to the prophet Ezekiel when, in his vision, the spirit took him and carried him away to see the people of the captivity at the Tel-abib, by the river Chebar. "Then the spirit took me up, and I heard behind me a voice of a great rushing, saying, Blessed be the glory of the Lord from his place. I heard also the noise of the wings of the living creatures that touched one another, and the noise of the wheels over against them, and a noise of a great rushing. So the spirit lifted me up and took me away, and I went in bitterness, in the heat of my spirit; but the hand of the Lord was strong upon me. Then I came to them of the captivity at the Tel-abib, that dwelt by the river of Chebar, and I sat where they sat, and remained there astonished

---

[10]Isa. 53:7, K. J. V.

among them seven days."[11]

People often say in Aramaic that "He has been seized by the spirit," meaning "He has been driven to act promptly." Or, they say: "The wind has entered into him," meaning "He is very hasty." The Aramaic word *ruha* means both "spirit" and "wind."

In Matthew's gospel, we are told that Jesus was led by the spirit to go to the desert. "Then was Jesus led up of the spirit into the wilderness to be tempted of the devil."[12] This means that Jesus felt an inner urge or prompting of the spirit to go to the nearby desert to try himself out.

When good things are done, people often say that the spirit is doing these things or making someone do them. At times, the spirit prevented the disciples from going to certain places. For example, when Paul and Silas wanted to visit Bithynia, the Spirit suffered them not to go.[13] In Luke's gospel we are told that Simeon "came by the Spirit into the temple," which means " he was led by God to enter the temple at a certain time."[14]

After the baptism of the Ethiopian eunuch, Phillip was "caught away" by the Spirit of the Lord. That is, he immediately took leave of the Ethiopian and began preaching the gospel in other cities where he had started to go before he met the eunuch. He was found later at Azotus. The high Ethiopian official had been converted and baptized so there was no reason for further delay. No doubt the eunuch was accompanied by a retinue of servants and other companions. Being occupied for a time, he soon found out that Philip had suddenly left him.

Jesus, prior to his resurrection, always walked from one place to another. His disciples did the same thing. There is no mention in the gospel that Jesus' disciples were carried by the spirit from one place to another or used any other means to travel. After his resurrection,

---

[11] Ezk. 3:12-15.
[12] Mt. 4:1, K. J. V.
[13] Acts 16:7.
[14] Lk. 2:25-27.

Jesus appeared to his disciples and disappeared suddenly. This was done after Jesus had arisen in a spiritual body[15] so that he could even enter a room when a door was closed and locked.

When we are engaged in God's work, doors open to us. We will meet people of prominence and the spirit of the Lord will lead and guide us in all matters. Being so guided, we will reach our destination promptly and safely.

---

[15]See 1 Cor. 15:35-44, especially verse 44.

CHAPTER 9

PAUL'S VISION

And he said, Who art thou, Lord? And the Lord said, I am Jesus whom thou persecutest; it is hard for thee to kick against the pricks. Acts 9:5.

Part 1—JESUS OF NAZARETH. When Paul fell to the ground and the heavenly light was shining all around him, he heard someone speaking to him. He wondered who was talking to him, so he asked: "Who are you my Lord?" The Aramaic text reads: "And our Lord said, I am Jesus of Nazareth whom you persecute."[1] Other texts of the book of Acts for some unknown reason have omitted "of Nazareth." Jesus would not have said "I am Jesus," because the name "Jesus" was a common one. In the Near East, when a man has a common name, it is usually connected with his father's name or the name of his village.

Jesus was known as "the prophet from Nazareth in Galilee." He was also called "the Galilean."[2] Matthew reports in his gospel that Jesus would also be called "a Nazarene," fulfilling a prophecy.[3] The Pharisees and scribes also called him a Galilean. They said: "No prophet shall arise from Galilee."

Philip also referred to Jesus as "of Nazareth." "Philip found Nathanael, and said to him, we have found that Jesus, the son of Joseph, of Nazareth, is the one concerning whom Moses wrote in the law and the prophets."[4] Jesus never denied his town nor the region where he was reared.

Part 2—THE PRICKS. "It is hard for thee to kick against the pricks" is an Aramaic saying. It means that when you strike another

---

[1] Acts 9:5, Aramaic Peshitta text, Lamsa translation.
[2] See Lk. 23:6.
[3] Mt. 2: 21-23. See Errico & Lamsa, *Aramaic Light on the Gospel of Matthew*, "Nazareth," pp. 29-30.
[4] Jn. 1:45, Aramaic Peshitta text, Lamsa translation.

person, you may hurt yourself. Throughout the Near East, hornets, mosquitoes, and other insects are often killed by catching them in your hands and squashing them or by hitting one's hand against the wall where they have alighted. When the hornet is struck, the stinger may stick in the hand and cause inflammation. When disturbed, some of these insects try to sting their attacker. People often say: "You have made them like hornets," meaning "you have antagonized them or made them bitter."

Prior to his conversion, Paul thought of the Jews who were embracing Jesus' message as thorns, hornets, and bees that annoy and pester people. The Jewish followers of Jesus were a great annoyance to the high priests, Pharisees, and the Jews who were extremely zealous for their religion and traditions. These groups were opposed to all changes and reforms.

Paul thought that the sooner he could get rid of Jesus' disciples and followers the better it would be for everyone. But he did not realize what the consequences would be. By persecuting and killing these believers of the new gospel, Paul was creating more interest in Jesus' message and was actually helping to spread his teachings. It was also arousing some of the people's disapproval of the established religious system that Paul was representing. When the converts were accused and brought before judges and governors, they had an opportunity to testify to the truth and make Jesus' teachings known.

There are certain principles and unseen forces at work here. What one sows, one also reaps, and he who takes up the sword and uses force will perish by the sword. Thus, the spirit of Jesus was warning Paul in a vision. Paul's violent acts against those who believed in Jesus' gospel would only bring about unfavorable results that would hurt him. Now he began to realize that persecution could not hinder nor rid the land of Jesus' followers.

The murderous mission that Paul had embarked upon was not an easy task. Zealous as he was, he began regretting his actions and the false testimonies against those who were practicing Jesus' teachings. He witnessed with his own eyes how these people, who were suffering and dying, were praising God and confessing Jesus' name.

They did not curse their enemies for the unjust persecutions they were experiencing. Seeing these things made Paul reconsider his actions.

JESUS WARNED PAUL

And the men which journeyed with him stood speechless, hearing a voice, but seeing no man. Acts 9:7.

Kala in Aramaic means "sound, noise or voice." When one wishes to use the term "speech" or "a talk," then the Aramaic word *mamla* is used. In this verse, the author says that the men who were with Paul heard a voice when Jesus spoke to him. But Acts 22:9 reads that the men saw the light but "they heard not the voice."

These two verses, Acts 9:7 and Acts 22:9, seem to contradict one another but, in fact, they do not. Both Paul and his traveling companions heard the voice and fell to the ground, but his companions did not recognize or understand what was taking place. They were frightened and confused. To them it may have been like a clap of thunder or some sort of noise or sound. Others also might have heard the voice but couldn't grasp what was being said; Paul, however, having a guilty conscience, understood what Jesus said to him.

There is a strong probability that just a few minutes before he heard the voice, Paul was thinking about his persecutions against Jesus' disciples. He had seen and heard Stephen delivering his wonderful speech in which he sought to prove that Jesus was the promised Messiah. He had watched Stephen die a horrible death and heard him say a prayer of forgiveness instead of cursing those who were stoning him. Undoubtedly, the scene made a great impression on him. Paul had arrested and persecuted many men and women and had been impressed with their great faith and loyalty to their master, Jesus of Nazareth.

Now Paul had come to himself. He had discovered that he was wrong in persecuting the disciples of Jesus. The words uttered by Jesus were meant for Paul only. That is why the others who were with him did not understand what was said.

SPIRITUAL BLINDNESS

And he was three days without sight, and neither did eat nor drink. Acts 9:9.

Travelers in the Arabian desert, the Sudan, and other hot countries are often blinded by the sun's rays. Today, Englishmen and other Europeans, when traveling in these countries, wear dark glasses to protect their eyes. In the past, before dark glasses were invented, people suffered terribly from the brilliant rays of the sun. Even now, Arabs and other native travelers are often stricken by the sun during the hot summer months. The heat is so intense and the sun's rays so bright that it's difficult to lift up one's head.

Some people say Paul was stricken by the sun's rays. Arabian historians relate similar cases of people being blinded by the sun. But in the third verse of this chapter we are told that "suddenly there shone round about him a light out of heaven." Paul was blinded in a mysterious way; no one knows exactly what happened except Paul himself.

For years he had been blind to the truth of Jesus' gospel of the kingdom. He had been instrumental in attacking his disciples, breaking up their meetings, burning their books, and bringing men and women to trial. Now he was temporarily struck blind so that his eyes might see a new world. The old vision, derived from the traditions of the elders, was completely destroyed. Up until this time, Paul had known nothing but theological debates and arguments that he had been taught in his youth. Now he was to see truth in a new way and with a new vision.

People often become blind by their own physical and material desires. Nevertheless, some come to themselves in due time. Their eyes become open and they begin to reason and see things differently. There are those, of course, who have perfect vision but, at times, cannot really see what is around them. For example, when Hagar and her son were dying from thirst, she could not see the well that was nearby. No doubt, her temporary blindness was from harboring bitterness in her mind against Sarah, her former mistress. Nonetheless, when she began praying, her spiritual senses were restored and she could now see the well that saved her and her son.[5]

PAUL GIVEN AUTHORITY

And here he hath authority from the chief priests to bind all that call on thy name. Acts 9:14.

The Jewish high priest had no temporal jurisdiction over Syria, but, as a spiritual leader, he exercised religious authority over all Jewish people throughout the Roman Empire and other parts of the world. Nonetheless, his political authority was limited to the province of Judea.

At this time, Syria was under a governor-general whose seat was at Antioch. Syria was occupied by the Romans during their conquest of the Near East, about 67 BCE. This region was of military importance because it was close to the borders of the Parthian Empire.

The high priest as an ethnarch—that is, the head of the Jewish race—could appeal to the Roman authorities in Syria through the procurator at Jerusalem. Then the procurator would consult the governor-general at Antioch or other high Roman officials stationed at Caesarea. The Romans did everything possible to please the Jews so that they could collect their taxes. Without Roman approval, Paul could not have gone to Damascus on such a mission.

A similar situation existed in the past century. Leaders of minority groups in Syria and Iraq had positions similar to that which the Jewish high priest held under the Romans. They exercised religious jurisdiction over their people, who lived under separate mandates. At times they obtained letters from one governor-general

---

[5]Gen. 21:14-20.

to another.

Paul's authority was limited to the Jews who lived in Damascus. He had no power to interfere with people of other races who had embraced the teachings of Jesus. Having obtained authority from the Romans and supplementary documents from the Jewish high priest, he could close down their meeting places and arrest Jews who had become disciples of the new gospel. He could bring them back to Jerusalem to be tried before the council—that is, the Sanhedrin.

SCALES

And immediately there fell from his eyes as it had been scales: and he received sight forthwith, and arose, and was baptized. Acts 9:18.

Kalpeh is the Aramaic word for "scales." It means "a thin layer of skin." We do not know exactly how Paul became blind, but we are sure that he could not see until Ananias laid his hands on him and restored his sight.

An individual who is full of hatred and revenge is often referred to as blind. Spiritual blindness sometimes causes physical blindness. Aramaic speaking people usually say, "his eyes have darkened so that he cannot see." This saying means that the person is misled by false notions, hatred and anger.

Paul's blindness was symbolic of the doubt that had plagued him for many years. He had been searching for truth, but his mind was closed by false pride, literalism, and traditions. These things created a psychological veil that hung over his eyes and blinded him. On his way to Damascus his blindness became more acute until finally he lost his vision completely and had to be helped by the men who journeyed with him.

The scales that fell from his eyes were symbolic of traditions and dogmas that had obscured his sight and understanding of the real truth and led him to persecute Jesus' disciples and followers. Now his physical sight was restored and his eyes were opened for the first time to understand the meaning of religion. Long held cultural and religious traditions vanished from his mind. The tenacious grip of the past was broken and no longer held him. Everything disappeared before the truth that now filled his mind. It all went like a shadow that disappears before the light. His physical blindness was temporary. It was to serve the purpose of awakening his consciousness to truth and making him a loyal disciple of Jesus.

LET DOWN FROM THE WALL

Then the disciples took him by night, and let him down by the wall in a basket. Acts 9:25.

Generally, houses in Damascus and other ancient towns and cities in Syria and Palestine are one-story structures. Large houses have an inner courtyard and stairs that lead to the roof. In that part of the world, housetops are used for drying vegetables and wheat, as playgrounds for children, and as meeting places for men. Jesus often spoke about housetops. "And let him that is on the housetop not go down into the house."[6] On another occasion he told his disciples that what he was saying to them secretly they, in turn, must preach from the housetops.

Some houses are built close to the city gate. Others adjoin the city wall. Rahab, the harlot, concealed Hebrew spies under the stalks of flax she was drying on the housetop that adjoined the city wall.[7] David was likewise let down through a window when he escaped from king Saul.[8] Paul refers to his escape in his second epistle to the Corinthians: "And through a window in a basket was I let down by the wall and escaped his hands."[9]

---

[6]Mk. 13:15-16.
[7]See Joshua 2:15.
[8]See 1 Sam. 19:12.
[9]2 Cor. 11:33.

GRECIAN JEWS

And he spake boldly in the name of the Lord Jesus, and disputed against the Grecians: but they went about to slay him. Acts 9:29.

The Aramaic text reads: "And he spoke openly in the name of Jesus, and debated with the Jews who understood Greek."[10] The term "Grecians" is incorrectly applied here. The Aramaic word for Greeks is *Yonayeh*. *Yownaeeth* is a verbal noun with an adverbial form that refers to the language of the people—that is, the Greek language.

Josephus, the famous Jewish historian of that day, circa 44 CE, in his book of Jewish wars, states that Greek was not spoken in Palestine and that there were only a few men who had tried to learn this language.[11] Nevertheless, there were Jews from Alexandria, Greece, and Rome who came every year to Palestine to worship. These Jews were liberal in their religious concepts and could speak Greek. Jews from foreign lands usually spoke several languages in addition to their own tongue.

Paul was educated as a Pharisee and from his boyhood grew up in Jerusalem. The Pharisees were opposed to reforms, strange customs and foreign languages, especially Greek. Paul, like Josephus, knew some Greek. Nevertheless, speaking a foreign tongue and being able to write it are two different things. It is easier to learn to speak a language than it is to read and write it.

TABITHA RAISED

But Peter put them all forth, and kneeled down, and prayed; and turning him to the body said, Tabitha, arise. And she opened her eyes: and when she saw Peter she sat up. Acts 9:40.

In most of the houses in biblical lands there is little or no privacy

---

[10] Acts 9:29, Aramaic Peshitta text, Lamsa translation.
[11] See *Antiquities* xx, xi, 2.

A small house, fourteen by twenty-four feet, is often occupied by two, three or more families. This makes it very difficult for any who are sick or who seek quietness and peace. When a member of a family is ill, the house becomes crowded with relatives, neighbors and other visitors from the town and from nearby villages.

On such occasions, friends, relatives and even enemies come to see the sick person whom they fear may die. The patient is never left at peace. Every visitor expresses grief, sheds copious amounts of tears and lectures to the patient, thus worsening the situation and frightening the sick individual.

The house is constantly filled with noise and confusion and when the patient is dying, he is removed to a closet in the corner, where the mourners and professional singers gather around him. The younger people and children are asked to leave the house and stay out. When a person dies late in the afternoon, the corpse is put in a little room or is taken to the church for the night. The people consider leaving the body in the house as unclean. Burial takes place the next day.

Simon Peter ordered the professional mourners and the visitors out of the room. Sometimes, healers throw themselves down beside the bed and pray aloud with tears. Other healers touch the body of the person to see whether that person is really dead. Elijah stretched himself over the body of the widow's son as he prayed for life to be restored to the young lad. Such acts cannot be done before a crowd, especially in the case of a female patient.

Simon Peter knelt down by the body and prayed. Then he probably used some Aramaic expressions similar to those that Jesus used when he raised the daughter of Jairus: *"Talita qumi,"* meaning "Little girl, get up," or "arise!" Simon spoke her name "Tabitha" (pronounced *Tweetha* in Aramaic). It means "Gazelle." She awakened from her death sleep and sat up. Jesus' disciples were endowed with power to raise the dead, restore the mentally and emotionally ill and to cleanse people of skin disorders. There are other cases like this recorded in scripture where apostles and men of God brought the dead back to life.

CHAPTER 10

CONVERSION OF CORNELIUS

There was a certain man in Caesarea called Cornelius, a centurion of the band called the Italian band. Acts 10:1.

Cornelius was a captain of a Roman regiment called "The Italians." The Romans had several Italian regiments stationed in Syria and Asia Minor and a small garrison in Palestine. The rest of the Roman army that maintained order in the Eastern provinces was composed of native soldiers and mercenaries.

Prior to World War II, England had a few army regiments scattered in various parts of the Near East. These were divided into companies and stationed together with native soldiers at strategic places in Iraq and Egypt. However, the British did not interfere with the native governments and their civil functions. British officers often entered Christian churches to pray, especially in cities where there were no churches of their own denominations. This was also true of the Russian soldiers when stationed in Persia.

Cornelius had spent considerable time in Palestine and lived among the Jews. He was married and had children to care for but no place of worship of his own. That is to say, the Romans had no temples and did not have army chaplains as we do today. The soldiers and their officers were free to do whatever they pleased in regard to matters of faith and worship.

It seems most likely that Cornelius was a proselyte who had been a regular attendant of the local Jewish synagogue but was seeking something deeper than what was being offered. Cornelius had heard about Jesus, his teachings and miracles. He had also seen some of the great works that some of his disciples and followers were doing. God revealed to him the true way, the faith that Jesus taught. This was done through the vision that Cornelius saw when he was praying. He was earnestly seeking God's direction and guidance.

DREAMS AND VISIONS

He saw in a vision evidently about the ninth hour of the day an angel of God coming in to him, and saying unto him, Cornelius. Acts 10:3.

In Arabia messages were carried by word of mouth and by couriers whose task was to take written news from one town to another. This ancient method of communication still prevails in some areas of the Near East, but it is inadequate. At times friends and relatives living a short distance from each other cannot easily communicate with one another. Therefore, they constantly think of each other and rely on dreams and visions for information about each other's welfare. Many women and men claim to have seen angels and to have conversed with them.

The belief in visions and angelic visitations is so firmly established that people do not hesitate to carry out instructions that are revealed to them in their dreams. Everything is taken at face value. Warnings and bad omens often prevent caravans from leaving a town, or even discourage men and women from buying and selling. It frequently happens that as two persons are thinking of each other, both of them see a vision on the same day or night.

Cornelius was eager to receive the gospel according to Jesus. He was a member of the Jewish faith, but evidently he had not found full satisfaction. He had heard about Jesus, his healing power and some of his teachings. He did not know how to get in touch with those who were in possession of his gospel to ask them to share it with his household; being a Gentile and an army officer, his task was difficult and peculiar. The government was deliberately trying to stamp out this new movement. This made it difficult for him to approach Jesus' disciples, who he thought might suspect his sincerity.

At last Cornelius was guided and directed by God in his effort to contact Simon Peter, who at this time was staying at the house of Simon the tanner, at Joppa. The Lord had revealed to Peter through a daytime vision that he should not be afraid to go to Caesarea with three strangers who would come calling on him. Peter was not to refuse Cornelius' invitation. He was to teach Cornelius and his household the new gospel. The Gentiles were also to be given an opportunity to share in the kingdom of God.

Peter was convinced and obeyed the spiritual vision and commission. He immediately came down from the rooftop and was met by the messengers who had been sent by Cornelius. They told him of the vision that Cornelius had seen. Simon Peter then departed with them and went to Caesarea.[1]

A TRANCE

On the morrow, as they went on their journey, and drew nigh unto the city, Peter went up upon the housetop to pray about the sixth hour: And he became very hungry, and would have eaten: but while they made ready, he fell into a trance. Acts 10:9-10.

Modern canning, refrigeration and other scientific methods of preserving food were unknown in Palestine until the early 1900s and in some Near Eastern areas they are still not known. But, even in ancient times, these people knew how to preserve certain vegetables and fruits by sun-drying. However, where modern methods have not been introduced, bread and other foods are prepared fresh daily, even though cooking is a difficult task and the family supply is often insufficient from day to day.

Bread and other foods are baked in an earthen oven dug in the ground floor of the house. Most Eastern homes consist of one large room that the people use for a kitchen, a living room, bedroom, and guest room and in some regions it is shared by animals and chickens.

Usually, very early in the morning, an elderly woman rises first, mixes the dough and leavens it. Then she fires the oven with grass, manure or wood. Women in other homes also rise and light their ovens and soon every house becomes an inferno, filled with heat and smoke. The other occupants of the house are wakened and rise

---

[1]See Acts 10:19-23.

quickly and leave the house. Little children cry and everything is in some confusion until the cooking and baking are over.

In the Near East, it is not unusual for people to wait for five or six hours before dining. Generally, the family supply of bread has been exhausted during the evening meal. Sometimes this is caused by the arrival of unexpected guests late at night. When an important guest is entertained, many townspeople gather in the house of the host and are fed also. On the other hand, Semites eat very little in the morning. Half a loaf of bread, a slice of cheese, or a bowl of curds (buttermilk) is sufficient for a breakfast. When other food is scarce, nothing but bread can be served and the guests and family members must wait until the day's supply of bread is baked.

While women are baking bread and preparing the meal, the men impatiently wait on the housetop to escape the smoke and to pass the time. Housetops serve as playgrounds for children and meeting places for the adults. Hungry persons, every once in a while, look down the chimney in the center of the roof to see if the women are through cooking and the table ready.

The long waiting and the aroma of the fresh baked bread or other food comes up with the smoke, increasing their hunger. Every minute seems like an hour, especially to guests who have arrived late and have had nothing to eat since breakfast. Religious men, while waiting on the roof, say their prayers when the hour for prayer comes. Pious men pray four or five times a day.

Simon Peter had been staying at Simon's house as a guest. Evidently, his host had received other guests so that he was short of bread. Peter was so hungry that he easily fell into a faint or a trance. While he was in an ecstatic state of consciousness, he saw a large sheet coming from the sky, full of animals and all sorts of creeping things.

The vision was an answer to the prayer of Cornelius and to the Gentile issues that were soon to be raised in the new spiritual movement. It revealed that all humans were equal in God's sight and that the Gentiles were also invited to enter and participate in the kingdom of God.

UNCLEAN FOOD

And saw heaven opened, and a certain vessel descending unto him, as it had been a great sheet knit at the four corners, and let down to the earth: Acts 10:11.

The Aramaic word *shmaya* has several meanings, such as "sky, heaven, universe, or cosmos." In this instance, it means "sky." The Aramaic word *mana*, which has been translated as "vessel" in the King James Version of Acts, really describes a peculiar object. It refers to something of unfamiliar quality, form and size. The Aramaic text reads: "And he saw the sky open and something fastened at the four corners, resembling a large linen cloth. . . ."[2]

Poor families, who cannot afford to own a copper tray, serve their food in a piece of cotton cloth about a yard square. The cloth is spread on the floor before the seated guests. Dishes containing food and loaves of bread are placed on the cloth. In Aramaic the cloth is called *supra* or *patora*.

When Simon fell into the trance, he was hungry and was expecting to be called at any minute to go down to eat. In this state he saw a heavenly vision—a large tablecloth hanging from the sky, full of all kinds of beasts and reptiles, unholy and unclean to the eyes of a devout member of the Jewish faith. He was mystified by the dreadful and atrocious sight. He didn't understand the meaning of his vision until the messengers who had been sent by Cornelius arrived and told him about Cornelius' vision. Then Peter was directed to proceed quickly to Caesarea, the capital of Roman Palestine.

Simon Peter was a Galilean but a Jew by faith. The Jews were not only prohibited from eating certain animals that the Gentiles ate, but they also had no social dealing with pagans, especially the Romans and Greeks. At the outset Peter hesitated to preach to the Gentiles, particularly the Romans. Both he and Cornelius were spiritually guided to meet for a common purpose.

---

[2]Aramaic Peshitta text, Lamsa translation.

The Jews had classified many animals, birds and certain kinds of fish as "unclean." Gentiles made no such distinction. By means of Peter's vision, what human beings had declared "unclean" were shown to be clean in God's sight. God had created everything for a good purpose. The four-footed beasts were symbolic of the Gentiles, whom the Jews regarded as "unclean." But God considered the Gentile people as clean.

The four corners of the cloth denote the four corners of the earth. Up until that time, the teachings of Jesus had reached only Galileans, Jews and Samaritans, but now it was to be declared to people of all races throughout the world. Jesus had told them that his gospel of God's kingdom should be taught and practiced among all nations, beginning at Jerusalem.[3]

GENTILES INVITED

But Peter said, Not so, Lord: for I have never eaten any thing that is common or unclean. Acts 10:14.

Mosaic law prohibited the eating of certain animal meats, birds and other creeping things. For example, animals whose hoofs were not split or animals whose hoofs were parted but who did not chew their cud were declared unclean. Nevertheless, some animals who chewed their cud but whose hoofs were not divided were lawful to eat. But swine, whose hoofs are divided but who do not chew their cud were declared unlawful.[4]

All species that crawled on four feet were declared unclean.[5] The law specified in detail what Jewish people were to eat and what they were not to eat. Near Eastern Christians and Muslims still keep the Mosaic law. They refrain from eating animal meat that is forbidden by the law.

---

[3]Lk. 24:47.
[4]Lev. 11:1-7.
[5]Lev. 11:20.

Simon Peter was a strict follower of the Mosaic law. He had never eaten anything that had been declared unlawful. It was difficult for him to depart from the customs and traditions of his people.

The unclean creatures that Peter saw in his vision symbolized the Gentiles with whom the Jews refused to associate.[6] But now they were declared clean. The old covenant had been given to the Jews in preparation for God's mission. This new covenant under Jesus was given to all nations. From the very beginning God had not discriminated against the Gentiles, for they, too, were his children.[7]

SYMBOLOGY

Now while Peter doubted in himself what this vision which he had seen should mean, behold, the men which were sent from Cornelius had made enquiry for Simon's house, and stood before the gate. Acts 10:17.

In some visions the meaning of the dream is clearly told to the recipient by the spoken word. The person hears a voice and may even hold a conversation with God or the angel (messenger) in the dream. Other visions come just with symbols. A few examples of these kinds of visions are: Jacob's vision of the ladder,[8] Joseph's dream of the sheaves of wheat, the sun, moon and stars,[9] and Pharaoh's dream of seven fat and lean cows.[10]

Many such visions occur in the prophetic writings of Isaiah, Ezekiel, Daniel, Hosea and other books in the Bible. Some of these dreams are difficult to decipher and understand. One has to know the meaning of the symbols in order to interpret them. This is the reason many people sought the help of wise men and dream interpreters and, at times, were doubtful about the meaning of a dream until it could

---

[6]Acts 10:28.
[7]Acts 10:34-35.
[8]Gen. 28:12.
[9]Gen. 37:5-11.
[10]Gen. 41:1-4.

be explained.

Pharoah and Nebuchadnezzar did not rest until they found wise men to interpret their dreams. The Egyptian and Chaldean wise men often could not decipher the meaning of the symbols, but Joseph and Daniel had the ability to decode them. Sometimes a complicated and mysterious dream will be revealed through a second dream. For example, when Daniel could not understand certain symbols in the first vision he had received, he prayed, and then the secret was disclosed in a second dream.[11]

Simon Peter doubted the value of his vision because he could not understand its meaning. Everything in his daydream was contrary to his religious upbringing. However, when the men who were sent by Cornelius arrived, Peter was convinced that God had called him to preach Jesus' gospel of the kingdom to the Gentiles.

WORSHIPING SIMON PETER

And as Peter was coming in, Cornelius met him, and fell down at his feet and worshipped him. But Peter took him up, saying, Stand up; I myself also am a man. Acts 10: 25-26.

According to Near Eastern custom, when people meet a holy man or a high government official, they bow down to him as a sign of respect. The Aramaic word *saghad* and the Arabic word *sajad* mean "to bow down in respect." The more important the person, the lower one has to bow.

For example, for a king or a prince, the people bow until their foreheads touch the ground. Many Near Eastern Christians and all Muslims, when praying, kneel and bow until their foreheads touch the ground. This is the reason Cornelius bowed to the ground before Peter's feet.

Cornelius was not really worshiping Peter as one would worship God; he was paying homage to the man of God who had been a

---

[11]Daniel 8:15-27.

disciple of Jesus. But Peter, a true disciple of Jesus, did not want this high government official to bow to him. Jesus had told his disciples that the greatest among them was to be a servant of all, showing true humility. Therefore, Peter declined the honors and the glory that were sought by religious and political men of his day.

Other religious men demanded such homage from their followers, especially in religions that recognized an emperor as their god. Peter was no demigod and he didn't want Cornelius to pay him such honors.

THE GALILEAN MOVEMENT

That word, I say, ye know, which was published throughout all Judea and began from Galilee, after the baptism which John preached.
Acts 10:37.

The movement that Jesus of Nazareth initiated, and which has been named Christianity, began in Galilee. Jesus came down from his home town of Nazareth and was baptized by John in the river Jordan in Judea. After his baptism he went into the Arabian desert where he fasted for forty days.[12] From there he returned to Galilee where he immediately announced God's kingdom and gathered disciples and followers. His spiritual mission and movement had now begun.

Most of the three years of Jesus' ministry were spent in the town by the lake of Galilee and in Syria. His disciples and his first followers were all Galileans. Jesus made several visits to the holy city, where he preached in the courtyard of the temple. He also preached in the marketplaces and in the homes of people, but his starting point was Galilee, to which he always returned. He was not welcome in Judea.

Simon gave Cornelius a brief historical summary of the new faith that Jesus taught, the life of its founder, the miracles and wonders he had performed, and the tragic death he had met. Peter

---

[12]Mt. 4:1-2.

was proving to Cornelius that Jesus was the promised Messiah who had been rejected by the Jewish religious authorities and who now had opened the door for the Gentiles to enter God's kingdom. Cornelius had heard of Jesus and the many miracles and wonders he had wrought. He wanted to hear some news firsthand from a man who had been with Jesus from the beginning of his ministry and who was an authority.

THE CROSS

And we are witnesses of all things which he did both in the land of the Jews, and in Jerusalem; whom they slew and hanged on a tree: Acts 10:39.

The Aramaic word for tree is *elana*. But the word used in this text is *kessa* and it means "dry wood" or "a piece of wood." Therefore, according to the Aramaic text, what Peter means is that Jesus was crucified on the cross.
When a man was crucified, he was stretched out on the cross and his hands and feet were fastened with nails. Jesus was not hanged on a tree or tied to a piece of wood as a few biblical teachers and some European writers and artists have depicted his crucifixion.
"And he bore all our sins, and lifted them with his body on the cross."[13] The Aramaic word used by Peter in this verse is *sleewa*, meaning "cross." *Kessa* is a general term and is used in some cases, as in Acts 5:30. But *sleewa* is generally used when the form of the cross is described.

JUDGE OF THE LIVING AND THE DEAD

And he commanded us to preach unto the people, and to testify that it is he which was ordained of God to be the Judge of quick and dead. Acts 10:42.

---

[13] 1 Peter 2:24, Aramaic Peshitta text, Lamsa translation.

According to the gospel of John, on the last day Jesus is to judge both the living and the dead. The dead will rise and together with the living will come before the judgment seat to answer for their deeds. Jesus said: For the Father judgeth no man, but hath committed all judgment unto the Son."[14]

Scripture tells us that the good and the bad will be separated, as a shepherd separates the sheep from the goats and as a farmer separates the tares from the wheat. It is people's own evil devices that separate them from others. At the end, truth will expose the forces of evil and evil will destroy itself.

---

[14] n. 5:22, K. J. V.

CHAPTER 11

EATING WITH GENTILES

And when Peter was come up to Jerusalem, they that were of the circumcision contended with him, Saying, Thou wentest in to men uncircumcised, and didst eat with them. Acts 11:2-3.

In the Near East, members of rival religions never associate with one another even when they live under the same roof. They never share meals together. Every faith has its own ordinances, customs and food laws. People in this respect are governed by traditions and the dictates of their hearts. The state seldom interferes in religious matters.

For example, a Muslim never eats meat if the animal has been slaughtered by a Jew or Christian. Many Near Eastern Christians do not eat bread baked by Jews. Jewish people are prohibited from eating meat in the home of a Christian. The reason for this is that a Jew cannot eat meat that has not been properly slaughtered and cleaned according to the Kosher laws.

Peter was rebuked by Jewish followers of Jesus for eating with Gentiles. It was Peter who was the first apostle to admit Gentiles into the early gatherings of Jesus' disciples. This is the reason he ate with them. Paul has been credited as the apostle to the Gentiles, but it was Peter who began this work after he had received his vision.[1]

Jesus had healed and converted Gentiles, but he instructed his disciples to limit their activities for the time being to the Jews, Galileans and members of the Ten Tribes who had been scattered abroad. He did not want to offend the Jews by breaking their laws. He told his disciples to go to no one but the lost sheep of the house of Israel.[2] The seed (teaching) of Jesus' gospel was to take root first among Jewish people, then to spread throughout the Gentile world.

---

[1] Acts 10:9-43.
[2] Mt. 10:6.

At last the Holy Spirit had come to the Gentiles, who were invited to enter and participate in God's kingdom. From then on there would be neither Jew nor Gentile but only one family of believers in the teaching of Jesus. Doctrines and teachings concerning the truth of God that had been hidden in the Jewish faith were to be unveiled and shared with the Gentile world.

THE EARLY MISSIONS

Now they which were scattered abroad upon the persecution that arose about Stephen traveled as far as Phenice, and Cyprus, and Antioch, preaching the word to none but unto the Jews only. Acts 11:19.

The notion not to preach among Gentiles was based on an early teaching derived from Jesus' own command. Many descendants of the Ten Tribes and the Jews of the tribe of Judah were scattered in Syria, Cilicia, Cyprus and Asia Minor. Jesus' gospel of the kingdom was to be firmly established among them first, then among the Arameans and other Semitic peoples who were racially and geographically close to the Jews and Galileans. They all spoke Aramaic dialects and their customs and cultural backgrounds were very similar. This made it easier for the early missionaries to spread the gospel and establish their centers in Antioch, Damascus, Edessa, Babylon and Rome.

The apostles and their disciples were usually welcomed to speak in synagogues and homes. This was the experience of Paul during his journeys in Asia Minor and Greece. The Jews who were scattered among these places and others were friendly to the new missionaries. Jesus once had preached in the vicinity of Tyre and Sidon, thus introducing the Galilean movement into Syria. He had visited several Syrian cities and his fame had spread throughout that country. But the church in Antioch was founded by early Jewish disciples of Jesus who had fled from severe persecution in Palestine. Later Barnabas visited the city and was much encouraged by the progress the church was making. After having met Paul at Tarsus, he brought Paul with him to Antioch where both of them taught the people.

The disciples were first called *M'sheeheh,* "Christians" (literally "anointed ones") at Antioch. Before that they had been known as *Nasroyeh*—that is, "the followers of Jesus of Nazareth."

The work among the Greeks in Macedonia and Greece was very early indeed, but the gospel was not introduced into these countries by the twelve disciples themselves but by their converts, such as Paul, Luke, Barnabas and others. We must also understand that soldiers, prisoners, slaves and merchants who had accepted Jesus' gospel did their part in spreading his teaching wherever they went. Paul met many followers of Jesus on his journeys.

Acts 11:20 clearly explains that certain converts from Cyprus and Cyrene went to Asia Minor and preached among the Arameans, Greeks and other groups of people. In those early days every believer in Jesus as the Christ was a full-fledged missionary ready to sacrifice everything, even life itself, for the sake of the faith. This zeal and sincere devotion were extremely prominent during the period of widespread persecution of the early followers.

ANTIOCH IN SYRIA

And when he had found him, he brought him unto Antioch. And it came to pass, that a whole year they assembled themselves with the church, and taught much people. And the disciples were called Christians first in Antioch. Acts 11:26.

After the death of Alexander the Great, about 323 BCE, his kingdom was divided among his four generals. Antioch became the capital of what, in the second century BCE, was known as the Syrian kingdom. The Syrian kings persecuted the Jews, forced some of them to eat swine, and defiled the temple in Jerusalem. Under their rule, the Jews revolted and gained their freedom. The struggle between the Syrian kingdom and the new Jewish commonwealth under the Hasmonean dynasty continued until both Syria and Palestine were conquered by the Romans about 65 BCE.

In the days of its glory, Antioch was a rival of Alexandria, Athens, Seleucia, and other great cities in the East and West. The city was famed for its magnificent temple of Jupiter, theater and other beautiful buildings. It was a center of art and culture and a gateway to the East. During Roman occupation, Antioch became the seat of the Roman governor-general. The city was important both from a commercial and military point of view. The Romans had large garrisons and military supplies stored in the province of Antioch for their campaigns against Persia. For nearly five centuries, the city remained the spearhead of the Roman armies and a base of operations. (Antioch in Syria, where the followers of Jesus were first called Christians, should not be confused with Antioch in Pisidia.)

After Stephen had been martyred, many of Jesus' disciples and followers fled to Antioch. The Christian church prospered there under the Romans. Thus Antioch became an important Christian center and the headquarters of the apostles. It was at Antioch that certain prophets and teachers laid hands on Paul and Barnabas and sent them on their missionary journey. For many centuries Antioch remained a strong evangelizing center. It sent missionaries both eastward into Persia and westward into the Roman Empire.

CHAPTER 12

HEROD AGRIPPA

Now about that time Herod the king stretched forth his hands to vex certain of the church. Acts 12:1.

Herod Agrippa was the grandson of Herod the Great, who was the son of Antipater, the founder of the Herodian dynasty. Antipater was an Idumean, who held an office under the Hasmonean kings. When the Romans conquered Syria and were exerting influence over the Jewish kingdom of Palestine, Antipater conspired against his master and as a reward was appointed procurator of Judea by Julius Caesar in 47 BCE.

The son of Antipater was made King of Judea by an act of the Roman senate, and was known as Herod the Great. To win the favor of the Jews and to establish his rule over them, he erected the magnificent temple in Jerusalem that became the center of worship until it was destroyed by Titus. Herod's descendants ruled for many years after his death.

In this verse, King Herod refers to Agrippa I. He was a strict Jew by faith and very crafty, like his grandfather. He did everything possible to please the Jews. He was the father of King Agrippa II, by whom Paul was tried before he was sent to Rome.

Agrippa I was the first king to persecute the new movement now becoming known as the Christian church. He beheaded Jacob (James), the son of Zebedee, who at that time was the leader of the Apostles and disciples of Jesus.

THE MURDER OF JAMES

And he killed James the brother of John with the sword. Acts 12:2.

This James[1] should not be confused with James, the son of Alpheus, or with James, Jesus' brother, who played an important role in the Christian ministry. James, who was martyred, was the son of Zebedee, John's brother and one of the twelve apostles.

According to the gospels, James and John were among the first disciples and were closest to their Master. Jesus often took Peter, James and John with him during many private devotion times. They were together on the Mount of Transfiguration.[2] At the last supper, Jesus revealed to John which disciple was about to betray him.

After the resurrection, James (John's brother) and Peter succeeded Jesus and were looked upon as the leaders of the Galilean movement. As a relative, Jesus' brother James was consulted on church affairs. Both the government authorities and the Jews also regarded James as the leader of the new sect, known as Galileans. This is the reason Herod Agrippa put him to death.

Originally, Jesus' brother James was not a disciple. That is, he never traveled with his brother when he was alive and teaching. He became identified with the Christian movement after Jesus' resurrection and was later honored as an apostle, respected and revered by his brother's disciples and followers. At times, he seems to have been regarded as the leader of the Christian movement and as successor to James, the son of Zebedee.[3]

PRISONS

And when Herod would have brought him forth, the same night Peter was sleeping between two soldiers, bound with two chains: and the keepers before the door kept the prison. And, behold, the angel of the Lord came upon him, and a light shined in the prison: and he smote Peter on the side, and raised him up, saying, Arise up quickly. And his chains fell off from his

---

[1]The name "James" is not correct. All Aramaic and Greek texts say "Jacob" not "James." We use "James because the K. J. V. maintains the name "James."
[2]Mt. 17:1-2.
[3]See Gal. 1:19; 2:9.

hands. And the angel said unto him, Gird thyself, and bind on thy sandals. And so he did. And he saith unto him, Cast thy garment about thee, and follow me. Acts 12:6-8.

Part 1—CONDITIONS OF THE PRISONS. In the Near East, prisons are different from those of the Western world. Modern methods of sanitation are unknown in many areas. Prisoners sleep in a row close to each other, their feet in fetters and long chains hanging from their necks. During the day their hands also are chained. Those who are charged with grave offenses are securely chained and heavily guarded to prevent escape.

Prison buildings are not fortified. Prisoners who succeed in breaking their chains can easily escape. Generally, the buildings are very old, their walls weak and crumbling with decay and their roofs full of holes. Some of the stones in the walls can be removed easily to make a passage for escape. That is why prisoners are constantly chained and heavily guarded.

In many Near Eastern countries, when prisoners make a successful escape, the prison guards are either severely punished or put to death. The officials usually suspect their guards of taking bribes. Prison guards receive no salary. They live on bribes and gifts of money, food and clothing, which the prisoners offer in exchange for favors. At night, when the prisoners sleep, they remove their cloaks and shoes and use them as pillows. By so doing, they protect their clothes from the guards who might steal them. They lie on the ground with the rest of their clothes on.

Part 2—PETER FREED BY A MESSENGER (ANGEL). A messenger sent from God touched Peter on his side to awaken him. As he arose, the chains fell off his hands. Peter then put on his upper garment and fastened his sandals on his feet, not fully realizing what was taking place. He probably was thinking that he was dreaming or seeing a vision. The doors of the large room where he was confined and the doors of the courtyard opened seemingly of their own accord.

Some biblical interpreters ascribe this miracle to an earthquake or some other natural phenomenon. It doesn't really matter how it happened. Even if the doors were opened by means of an earthquake, that would not minimize the importance of Peter's miraculous escape. The fact that it occurred at a time when Peter's life was in danger is in itself an intervention that saved his life. Undoubtedly, something beyond our understanding occurred while Peter was in prison

Similarly, Paul and Silas were delivered from the prison at Philippi. An earthquake shook the prison to its foundation. The doors were opened and their bonds loosened.[4] Jesus had promised his disciples that he would be with them always. He had assured them of spiritual guidance and protection.

GUARDIAN ANGEL

And when she knew Peter's voice, she opened not the gate for gladness, but ran in, and told how Peter stood before the gate. And they said unto her, Thou art mad. But she constantly affirmed that it was even so. Then said they, It is his angel. Acts 12:15.

The Aramaic word *malakha*, "angel," also means "messenger or minister." Semites of the Near East believe that every person has a guardian angel. They believe that everyone is entrusted by God to the care of an angel who advises and guides the individual in spiritual matters and cautions him or her about evil thoughts and actions.

Jesus warned his disciples not to despise little children because their angels stand in the presence of God. "For I say unto you, that in heaven their angels do always behold the face of my Father which is in heaven."[5] In heavenly realms, guardian angels act as people's representatives. Angels are spirits, that is, messengers from God, "who maketh his angels spirits; his ministers a flaming fire."[6]

The word for "angel" as used in this passage of the book of Acts may mean a "messenger." Those in the house thought that Peter

---

[4]See Acts 16:26-27.
[5]Mt. 18:10, K. J. V.
[6]Ps. 104:4.

might have sent them a message from prison. In the Near East, messengers are permitted to see prisoners and take them food; also, prisoners can send word by a messenger to friends, asking for money, food, and other things that are needed. John the Baptist had sent messengers to Jesus to ask him if he was the Messiah or if they should expect someone else.

The people in the house knew that Peter had been securely bound and heavily guarded. They doubted that he could have been released at such an early hour or that he could have escaped. This is the reason they did not believe the girl's report.

JAMES, THE BROTHER OF JESUS.

But he, beckoning unto them with the hand to hold their peace, declared unto them how the Lord had brought him out of the prison. And he said, Go shew these things unto James, and to the brethren. And he departed and went into another place. Acts 12:17.

James in this verse is Jesus' brother. Jesus' disciple James, the son of Zebedee and brother of John, was beheaded by Herod Agrippa I.[7] It seems that James, the brother of Jesus, was chosen to fill the vacancy made by the apostle's death. Matthias, in order to fulfill the number of apostles (12), was chosen to replace Judas Iscariot.[8] Therefore, James played an important part in the Christian ministry. Jesus had three other step-brothers who were known as Joses, Judah and Simon.[9]

When a dispute arose in the early church over circumcision, the matter was referred to the apostles in Jerusalem. Both Paul and Barnabas spoke before the apostles in defense of the Gentiles. When they were through with the discussion, James rose and spoke,

---

[7] Acts 12:2.
[8] Acts 1:2-26.
[9] Mt. 13:55; Mk. 6:3.

confirming what Peter had said in his address.[10] Both James and Peter were respected and honored as leaders. When Paul returned from his missionary journey in Asia Minor and Macedonia, he was received by James.[11] In his epistle to the Galatians, Paul says that when he went to Jerusalem, he saw only two apostles, Simon Peter and James, the brother of our Lord.[12]

Paul also relates how, when the men who were sent by James arrived in Antioch, Peter separated himself from the Gentiles because he feared the criticism of the Jewish Christians.[13] (See the comment on Acts 12:2, "The Murder of James.")

SMITTEN BY AN ANGEL

And immediately the angel of the Lord smote him, because he gave not God the glory: and he was eaten of worms, and gave up the ghost.
Acts 12:23.

Semites frequently use the expression "smitten by an angel," meaning "to become paralyzed." When pronouncing a curse on an enemy, a Semite may say: "May an angel smite you." When someone has been stricken by paralysis, people often report that the individual "has been attacked by an angel." At night, when people must cross a brook or a river, they call on God, fearing that they might be smitten by an angel as they cross over the stream of water.

"Eaten by worms" suggests that Herod suffered from a serious cancer. Semites did not know the names of diseases and germs. When speaking of a certain malady, they used terms that described vividly its nature. Herod had been persecuting the Church and had murdered one of the apostles. Now he, who had done so much evil to others, himself fell victim to a terrible disease.

---

[10] Acts 15:13.
[11] Acts 21:18.
[12] Gal. 1:18-19.
[13] Gal. 2:12.

CHAPTER 13

SIMON THE CARPENTER

Now there were in the church that was at Antioch certain prophets and teachers; as Barnabas, and Simeon that was called Niger, and Lucius of Cyrene, and Manaen, which had been brought up with Herod the tetrarch, and Saul. Acts 13:1.

"*Niger*" is an Aramaic name that means "carpenter." Simeon was called in Aramaic "Simon the carpenter." In colloquial speech *niger,* is often pronounced as *najjar*, that is, "one who works with wood."

Some Bible interpreters not knowing Aramaic or Arabic, think that this term meant a Negro or Black man. Today there are many preachers who use this word in their sermons, stating that a Negro helped Jesus carry his cross to Golgotha.[1] These preachers do not realize that the term "Negro" is derived from a Latin word and not a Semitic term.

In Mark 15:40, James the junior is called "James the less." A biblical commentator, taking this term very literally, instructs his readers that this James was a very short and small man. *Zora* in Aramaic means "younger," that is, "junior." Even today, if two men have identical names, one may be called *zora*, "the younger," and the other *gora,* "the older." At times, Near Easterners call men by the name of their occupation or some other association—Simon the tanner, Simon the leper, James the junior, Simon the elder—or women by the name of a town, such as Mary of Magdala.

SELEUCIA IN SYRIA

So they, being sent forth by the Holy Ghost, departed unto Seleucia;

---

[1] Lk. 23:26, Errico & Lamsa, *Aramaic Light on the Gospels of Mark and Luke,* "Bearing the Cross with Jesus," p. 265.

and from thence they sailed to Cyprus. Acts 13:4.

There are two cities that bear the same name: Seleucia in Mesopotamia and Seleucia in Syria. Both of these cities were named after Seleucus, one of the generals of Alexander the Great.

After the death of Alexander in 323 BCE, his kingdom was divided among his generals. Seleucus held much of the Eastern portion of the empire that embraced countries from India to Syria and Asia Minor. Seleucia in Mesopotamia was made the capital of the Eastern empire. The city is situated on the bed of the river Euphrates in lower Mesopotamia.

In the middle of the third century CE, Seleucia became the capital of the Sasanid dynasty and remained an important center of education and government until the seventh century, when the Arabs occupied it. Seleucia was also the seat of the ancient Church of the East and a great center of missionary enterprise. From there many missionaries went to Georgia, Turkistan, India and China.

The other Seleucia is not well known. It was a small city of much less importance, situated in Syria not far from Alexandretta and Antioch.

PREACHING IN SYNAGOGUES

And when they were at Salamis, they preached the word of God in the synagogues of the Jews: and they had also John to their minister. Acts 13:5.

Part 1—JEWISH CONVERTS. From the very onset of his missionary journey, Paul preached to the Jews in their synagogues. The people of other races who inhabited the island of Cyprus had not heard of this new movement. They were interested in their own religions.

Christianity was regarded as a Jewish movement that had its origin in Jewish Palestine. The Jews were well informed of political and religious changes that took place in their native land. They had heard of the teachings of Jesus and his death on the cross. Jewish synagogues were very liberal and sympathetic to Jewish travelers regardless of the various beliefs. They invited strangers of their own religion to speak, especially if they happened to come from Jerusalem.[2]

It was much easier for Paul and his companions to preach among people of their own race, religion, language and cultural background. When Paul succeeded in converting some of the Jews, these new followers of Jesus shared the gospel with their Gentile neighbors. "And as Paul and Barnabas were leaving them, the people besought them to speak these things to them the next Sabbath."[3]

Part 2—JOHN AS A MINISTER. John, who was also nicknamed "Mark,"[4] ministered to Paul and Barnabas in their missionary work. His duties were to carry the bag that contained books and food supplies for the journey, look for lodging, run errands, write letters and so on. However, while ministering to Paul and Barnabas, John Mark was preparing himself to become a preacher.

At that time, theological schools were unknown. Younger men received their education and discipline from older ministers. This custom still prevails among Assyrian Christians. Priests prepare and tutor laymen. On a missionary journey, the younger men also minister to their superiors' needs. John's position was similar to that of a deacon in the Assyrian Church of the East.

BAR-JESUS

And when they had gone through the isle unto Paphos, they found a certain sorcerer, a false prophet, a Jew, whose name was Bar-Jesus: Which was with the deputy of the country, Sergius Paulus, a prudent man; who called for Barnabas and Saul, and desired to hear the word of God.
Acts 13:6-7.

---

[2]Acts 13:15.
[3]Acts 13:42.
[4]Acts 12:25. See also Errico & Lamsa, *Aramaic Light on the Gospels of Mark and Luke,* "Introduction," pp. 1-4.

Sorcerers, magicians and astrologers were very popular in Near Eastern countries. Their company and advice were sought by kings, princes and governors. Some of them sat in the councils of state and were closely associated with the ruler, over whom they exerted tremendous influence. They counseled the leader on political and religious affairs, predicted periods of peace and prosperity and warned the people of impending disasters.

Pharaoh consulted his magicians on state matters. The Babylonian king, Nebuchadnezzar, depended on his soothsayers and fortune-tellers for help and explanations to carry out his expansion program to conquer the Near East.

Bar-Jesus means "son of Jesus." But the Aramaic text records a different name, *Bar-shuma*. He was a false prophet who had tremendous power over the governor of the island and his people. Undoubtedly this Jewish sorcerer debated with Paul and tried to prevent the governor from accepting Paul's teaching. He felt Paul's power, but he wanted to save his position and control.[5]

Paul rebuked Bar-shuma bitterly. The rebuke was so intense and powerful that it caused the sorcerer to temporarily lose his sight. His blindness to the truth resulted in physical blindness. Opposition to truth often can obscure one's vision and cause temporary blindness. Paul said to him, "Thou shalt be blind, not seeing the sun for a season," implying that the blindness would be of a short duration.

SAUL'S NAME CHANGED TO PAUL

Then Saul (who also is called Paul) filled with the Holy Ghost, set his eyes on him. Acts 13:9.

The name "Saul" in Semitic languages means "to ask." It is most probable that Paul was named after King Saul, who, like himself, was of the tribe of Benjamin.

In the book of Samuel we read that when Kish, Saul's father, had

---

[5] See Acts 13:8.

lost his donkeys, he sent his son, Saul, to find them. And while Saul was searching for them, he came to Rama and asked the prophet Samuel to help him find the donkeys. This name "Saul" might have been bestowed on Kish's son after this event because Samuel told him that he would soon be king over Israel.[6]

In the Near East, when a general triumphs in battle, he is usually given a new name. For example, General Inono, the former President of the Turkish Republic, was first known as Ismit Pasha, but when he defeated the Greek Army, he was given the name Inono, the namesake of the place of battle.

On the other hand, many biblical names indicate a great event that had taken place at the time the person was born. Also, when people change their religion, they frequently change their names. In the Near East, when a Christian becomes a Muslim, he is given a new name, usually the name of a great Muslim. But more times than not, they adopt the name of their prophet Mohammed.

Paul (Pul) is the name of an Assyrian King who invaded Israel in 771 BCE. Undoubtedly, Paul changed the name under which he had persecuted the disciples and followers of Jesus.[7]

PREACHING TO THE JEWS

Then Paul and Barnabas waxed bold, and said, It was necessary that the word of God should first have been spoken to you: but seeing ye put it from you, and judge yourselves unworthy of everlasting life, lo, we turn to the Gentiles. Acts 13:46.

Paul's and Barnabas' primary objective was to preach and teach the word of God among the people of their own race. The apostles had been instructed by Jesus to declare his gospel first to the tribes of Israel. Therefore, to make Jewish people disciples of the new gospel

---

[6]1 Sam. 9:1-20.

[7]This practice of changing names prevails today in America. When an African-American Christian becomes a Muslim, his name is changed to a Muslim name.

was their major effort. The Jews in those regions, who were so far from Palestine, were not thoroughly acquainted with the religious situation.

When the Jews invited Paul and Barnabas to speak, they were not aware of the purpose of their mission, nor did they expect them to preach Jesus' message of the kingdom. What the Jews wanted was a brief talk on Jewish history and some news about the Jews in Syria, Palestine and other regions where they had traveled. When they fully realized that Paul and Barnabas were preaching something new that was contrary to their understanding of Judaism, they became infuriated. They did not know that Paul and Barnabas were seeking to make them and their adherents disciples of Jesus' teaching. By the time they caught on to what these two men were doing, it was too late because their talks in the synagogues had already made an impression on many of their people.

When Paul began his address, the Jews listened and held their peace, but when they realized what he was saying, they rose up and tried to contradict him. Nevertheless, Paul's talk was successful.[8] A great number of Jews and many Gentiles had received and embraced Jesus' teaching, but Paul and Barnabas were thrown out of the city.[9]

---

[8] Acts 13: 14-46.
[9] Acts 13:48-50.

CHAPTER 14

SYNAGOGUE

And it came to pass in Iconium that they went both together into the synagogue of the Jews, and so spake, that a great multitude both of the Jews and of the Greeks believed. Acts 14:1.

Part 1—THE ORIGIN OF THE SYNAGOGUE. The Hebrew phrase *ohel moed*, "tent of meeting," more closely approximates the meaning of the Greek word *synagoge*. Most scholars believe that the synagogue originated in Babylon during the exile. Some biblical experts consider 2 Chronicles 17:9, "And they (Levites) . . . went about throughout all the cities of Judah and taught the people," as a possible clue to the beginning of the synagogue as an institution. However, Ezekiel 11:15-16 is usually cited as the first hint to the origin of the synagogue because of the Hebrew words *mikdash meaht*, translated as "little sanctuary." Regardless of when or how the synagogue did appear, it was an assembly and form of ceremonial worship where prayer, confession, and fasting were practiced but no animal sacrifices were offered. As the institution developed, scriptural passages were read and interpreted during the gatherings. The concept of the one universal God was promoted and maintained at synagogue meetings.

In this verse the Aramaic text reads: "And Paul and Barnabas entered into the Jewish synagogue and addressed the people in such manner that a great many of the Jews and of the Greeks believed."[1] The Jews adopted the synagogue as a place of assembly for worship and education during the Babylonian captivity. Before the destruction of the Jewish temple by the Chaldeans in 586 BCE, they worshiped at holy shrines and in the tabernacle designed by Moses.

King Solomon built the temple in Jerusalem circa 967 BCE[2] and

---

[1] Acts 14:1, Aramaic Peshitta text, Lamsa translation.
[2] 1 Ki. 6:1-38.

instituted a form of worship similar to that when Moses erected the tabernacle. The temple became a national shrine both for prayer and the offering of sacrifices. Consequently, Israel's religion was centralized in the southern kingdom of Judah. After the Chaldeans conquered the southern kingdom, sacrifices were discontinued, but the people maintained their religion and worship in designated meeting places, houses and other available sites.

About the year 450 BCE, the Jews returned from Babylon. Zorobabel, with the help of the Persian kings, built the second temple on the former site. Later, Herod the Great restored the temple to its former glory. Nevertheless, the Jews in villages, country places, and especially in foreign countries continued to worship in their designated meeting places that became known as synagogues. Every large village had a synagogue in which men and women assembled on the Sabbath Day to worship. During the feasts and other important occasions, however, they went to Jerusalem to worship and make offerings in the temple.[3]

The synagogue resembled the temple in many respects. It had a similar Menorah (golden candlestick) and scrolls, the Torah and the Prophets. Outstanding Torah teachers occupied the place of the priests, and the elders, the place of the Levites. The lessons were read from the books of the Torah and Prophets by a learned layman or a teacher.[4] (Interestingly, this custom is still observed by the Church of the East during its meetings. Lessons from the Hebrew Bible are read by a layman, epistles by a deacon, and the gospels by a priest.) The message, based on a text, was preached by an educated scholar or a lay teacher and then discussed by any scribes or learned men who happened to be present.

Generally, the portions of Scripture that were in Hebrew were interpreted in Aramaic. On a certain occasion, Jesus read the lesson and commented on it. "And he began to say unto them, This day is

---

[3] Lk. 2:22, 42.
[4] Lk. 4:16.

this scripture fulfilled in your ears."[5] The synagogue was an unadorned place of worship. There were no images or statues.

Adherents of the Jewish faith, whether strangers or members of the local congregation, were invited to speak after scriptural readings. Distant and isolated Jewish communities were always eager to hear news from Jerusalem. This is one reason why Paul was permitted to speak in so many synagogues on his journeys in Asia Minor and Greece. It is true that some of the Jews in Asia Minor and Greece were not aware of Paul's commission as a preacher of the gospel when they invited him to address the congregation. "And after the reading of the law and the prophets the elders of the synagogue sent to them, saying, O men and brethren, if you have a word of encouragement for the people, speak."[6]

The Jews, in this region, were very liberal and tolerant in the matter of worship. They let laymen and even strangers debate and express their opinions on different scriptural passages because the synagogue was also an educational center.

Part 2—GREEKS. In this instance, the reference to Greeks is correctly translated. The Aramaic word *yonayeh* means "Greeks." But the Aramaic term *ammeh* means "Gentiles," that is, kindred people in Palestine and Syria, like the Ammonites, Idumeans, Moabites and other people of Semitic origin but not of the twelve tribes of Israel.

There was a Jewish synagogue at Iconium, and Paul was invited to address the people. In this area the Jewish people were not conservative like the Jews in southern Palestine. Some of them were descendants of the Ten Tribes; others were generally discontent with the Jewish authorities; still others held liberal views concerning the Gentiles. That is why Paul was always welcome to speak there on the Sabbath. Such privileges were never granted in the synagogues in Palestine.

Apparently, a number of Greeks in Asia Minor, like some of the

---

[5]Lk. 4:21, K. J. V.
[6]Acts 13:15, Aramaic Peshitta text, Lamsa translation.

Syrians, had accepted the Jewish faith, probably a few as a result of intermarriage, some because of honest convictions, and others for various reasons. Many of these Greeks became converts to Jesus' gospel of the kingdom in the first century, but most of them had already been converted to Judaism before accepting the new teaching brought by Paul and others. Christianity began to spread among the pagan Greeks in the second and third centuries.

HUMAN GODS

And they called Barnabas, Jupiter; and Paul, Mercurius, because he was the chief speaker. Then the priest of Jupiter, which was before their city, brought oxen and garlands unto the gates, and would have done sacrifice with the people. Which when the apostles, Barnabas and Paul heard of, they rent their clothes, and ran in among the people, crying out. Acts 14:12-14.

Part 1—GREEK GODS. The Aramaic text reads: "So they called Barnabas the chief of the gods; and Paul they called Hermes, because he was the chief speaker."[7] In Aramaic the phrase *mareh alaheh* literally reads "Lord of the gods," that is, "the chief deity." Both Arameans and Greeks were idolaters in their religious concepts and worship. Deities of the more powerful tribes were given higher places in the temples and shrines. This was especially true of the gods of conquering races. At times, the emperors declared themselves gods and their images were venerated.

Jupiter is Latin for the Greek *Zeus*. He was the chief deity of the ancient Greek pantheon, the ruler of the heavens. He was also the god of the land, whose image was revered both by Greeks and other peoples in Asia Minor.

Images and idols represented the heavenly bodies that were worshiped by most of the pagan world. Prior to Hebrew monotheism, the sun, moon and stars were universally worshiped. Originally, the

---

[7]Acts 14:12, Aramaic Peshitta text, Lamsa translation.

images were made as tokens of honor to heavenly bodies, but centuries later this primitive notion was lost and the images themselves became the gods of the people.

The Hebrews also venerated and worshiped images on many occasions. It took their prophets many centuries to rid the land of idols of clay, stone, silver and gold. Gideon smashed the image that belonged to his father and destroyed its altar.[8] Elijah slew the prophets of Baal and destroyed their places of worship.[9]

The miraculous healing of the cripple who had been lame from birth made the people of Lystra regard Barnabas and Paul as "gods."[10] They were considered deified ambassadors The people called Barnabas "the chief god"—that is, Zeus—and Paul, "Hermes" (Latin—"Mercury"). Hermes was the messenger of the gods in the Greek Pantheon and the god who was the leader in speaking. Paul was a great thinker but not a fluent speaker. On one occasion Greek philosophers called him a chooser of words. Paul received his education in Jerusalem. He was well versed in Scripture and the Torah and he was the spokesman for the missionary work.

Part 2—PAGAN CUSTOM. The Aramaic text reads: "Then the priest of Zeus, whose shrine was outside the city, brought oxen and garlands to the gate of the courtyard where they stayed and he wanted to offer sacrifices to them." The offering of animals and food before shrines to holy men was common in many parts of the Near East until the mid 1950s. When sheiks, noblemen and other high secular and ecclesiastical officials travel, they are greeted by the people with offerings of animals, food and expensive garments as tokens of welcome, loyalty, and submission.

As a distinguished visitor approaches a town, the reception party kills an ox or a number of sheep in his honor. The meat is then eaten by the servants and hungry travelers and the remainder is distributed among the poor. On the arrival of some of these honored guests, a

---

[8] Judges 6:25.
[9] 1 Ki. 18:40.
[10] Acts 14:8-12.

lamb or sheep is slaughtered at the entrance of the house. Live sheep, oxen and horses are also given as gifts to highly honored guests. They do this because Near Easterners have plenty of animals but little cash. Some religious men and government officials often return home from a journey with many sheep, oxen, horses and other gifts.

To offer an animal before a religious personage is the highest token of loyalty and welcome one can extend. To entertain the guest and his many servants with an abundance of meat and bread is a very ancient custom. When God appeared to Abraham, the latter killed a calf and prepared food as a token of welcome.[11]

Paul, in his attempt to stop the priest from sacrificing to him and Barnabas, presents a short message about the true and living God. (See verses 15-17.) They didn't want this kind of honor.

Part 3—TEARING GARMENTS. Tearing one's clothes and cutting one's hair in mourning is very common among Semitic people. When they receive tragic news about the death of their relatives, men will tear their clothes and women cut their hair as a sign of deep grief and sorrow.

This custom still prevails among Near Eastern Arabs, Jews, Assyrians, and Kurds. Also when a man is accused of treason, he tears his garments to prove his innocence and to show protest. In such cases, the tearing indicates humiliation. When a person is humbled and severely punished, he is partially or completely stripped of his garments. When governors, noblemen and officials are demoted or dismissed on charges of treason and disloyalty, the royal robes, rings and other tokens of authority are taken from them. In some instances, the giver of a special garment removes it from the person who has been accused and tears it to shreds.

On the other hand, mentally ill people usually walk around naked. Mourners and accused men often become very violent and act insanely. In most cases, the garment is ripped open in front from the neck down. Kings and noblemen tear only a small part of their garment. King David and all the men who were with him tore their

---

[11]Gen. 18:6-7.

garments when they were informed about the death of King Saul and his son, Jonathan.[12] At times, mourners are prevented by friends from tearing their garments. Therefore, some mourners wait until their friends arrive before they make an attempt to tear their garments.

Paul and Barnabas tore their garments as a protest against those who proclaimed them "gods." By tearing their clothes, they emphatically declined the honor of being gods, proving that they were just men. Had they not done this, they would have been charged with treason by both the state and religious authorities for posing as gods.

Paul knew just how Easterners think and understood their temperament. He knew that such acts would not be tolerated by the priests and people in general. The crowd was moved by his speech, but the enthusiasm would not last long. Paul and Barnabas were preaching about the God of heaven and earth; they could not have accepted any honor that was contrary to Jesus' teaching.

ENTERING THE KINGDOM OF GOD

Confirming the souls of the disciples, and exhorting them to continue in the faith, and that we must through much tribulation enter into the kingdom of God. And when they had ordained them elders in every church, and had prayed with fasting, they commended them to the Lord, on whom they believed. Acts 14:22-23.

Part 1—TRIBULATION. Barnabas and Paul, like the disciples of Jesus, preached to the Jews who were scattered throughout Asia Minor. Many of these Jews, having to live among Gentiles and far from Jerusalem and their temple, readily embraced Jesus' gospel of the kingdom of God. They had been expecting the coming of the Messiah who would gather the scattered tribes from the house of Israel.

The Jewish authorities in Jerusalem were aware of this situation and were constantly in touch with the Jewish colonies through the

---

[12] 2 Sam. 1:11.

synagogues, warning them of the new religion that was rivaling them. They considered this new gospel as heresy and a departure from the doctrine of the elders and from the Torah and the Prophets. Paul, prior to his conversion, was commissioned by the high priest and the Sanhedrin in Jerusalem to go to Syria to stop the spread of the new movement in that land.

Paul and Barnabas knew Jesus' teaching: "Blessed are you when men reproach you and persecute you and speak against you every kind of evil, falsely, for my sake. Blessed are those who are persecuted for the sake of justice, for theirs is the kingdom of heaven."[13]

These two apostles, instead of promising the new disciples rich rewards in this life, told them the truth. They would suffer for accepting this gospel of the kingdom as the fulfillment of the old covenant. The leaders of the old covenant and the imperialists would do everything in their power to persecute the followers of Jesus. So it would be that with much tribulation—that is, trials, troubles and persecutions—the new disciples would enter the kingdom of God. Paul and Barnabas warned them of the thorny road upon which they were to travel because they knew that soon the religious authorities would renounce them from the synagogues.

Part 2—APPOINTING ELDERS AND TEACHERS. The Aramaic text reads: "And when they had ordained them elders (*kasheesheh*) in every church and had prayed with them with fasting, they commended them to our Lord, on whom they believed."[14] Appointing elders was an old Hebrew custom, inaugurated in the wilderness.[15] It acquired a new meaning during the Babylonian captivity and thereafter. At that time the synagogue took the place of the temple; the Aaronic priesthood came to an end, and a new system of priesthood was established with different functions from that of the old. This change occurred because the temple had been destroyed, most of the rituals discontinued and animal sacrifices abolished. The

---

[13]Mt. 5:10-11, Aramaic Peshitta text, Lamsa translation.
[14]Acts 14:23, Aramaic Peshitta text, Lamsa translation.
[15]Ex. 18:21.

people now were seeking spiritual truth in holy Scripture rather than mere formalism and literalism.

Elders were elected just like vestrymen in modern churches. The elders in turn elected a teacher, who acted as preacher and instructor in religious matters. Nevertheless some of the elders participated in services as they do even today in many ancient churches and synagogues in the Near East. They read the lessons and taught the people. When the head teacher was absent, one of the elders delivered an address.

In the Near East, elders devote most of their time to prayer and fasting. Some of them act as judges and arbitrators in religious and legal disputes. The people look to them for guidance in many matters, spiritual and political.

Paul and Barnabas appointed elders to take charge of small congregations to guide and teach them the true religion that Jesus taught.[16] At this time, converts were very few, books were scarce and false teachers of religion abounded. Elders were not needed to take charge of ritual and ceremonial practices, but they were to guard the congregations against false teachings, soothsayers and deceptive missionaries who would arrive after Paul and Barnabas departed.

In Hebrews 13:17 elders are referred to as leaders. In 1 Timothy and Titus, their office becomes more important; they are ordained by the laying on of hands. They must have certain qualities so that they might become teachers and guardians of the faith.[17]

NEW CHRISTIAN SEE[18]

And thence sailed to Antioch, from whence they had been recommended to the grace of God for the work which they fulfilled. Acts 14:26.

About 50 CE, Antioch in Syria became the new center of the

---

[16] Acts 20:17.
[17] 1 Tim. 3:1-2; Tit. 1:6.
[18] "See" is a church term meaning the center or seat of authority.

Church and of its missionary activities in Syria, the Persian empire, Asia Minor and other parts of the world. The martyrdom of Stephen and later that of James, the brother of John, sealed the fate of Jerusalem as the seat of Christianity.[19]

Antioch offered many advantages. Its geographical position made it a central place from which to spread the Jesus' gospel of the kingdom in Syria, Mesopotamia and Asia Minor. Jerusalem was far south; its environment was hostile to the new teaching and the Jewish authorities had some political power and influence in the province of Judea.[20]

Both Jews and Arameans in Antioch, Damascus and other Syrian cities were friendly to the new movement. Many of the Jews were descendants of the Ten Tribes. They were unfriendly to the Jews in the south. Antioch, because it was the seat of the Roman government in Syria, offered protection to the Christians. They were free to worship, teach and make new disciples.

In Jerusalem the Christians were still identified with the Jewish faith. They observed the Jewish law, ate specified food and dressed like the Judean Jews. These Jewish Christians demanded that the converts from among the Gentiles be circumcised and keep the law of Moses.[21] The Jewish authorities kept a watch on the new movement with much suspicion. They felt it was a menace to Judaism.

Thus Antioch became the major center for the Church throughout the world. From Antioch, Christian missionaries went into both the East and the West, making disciples of the people in both the Persian and Roman empires. For many centuries Antioch remained a major Christian center. By the fourth century, Antioch was noted for its theological schools and other institutions of learning. Today the city is still the seat of the Malkites, one of the branches of the ancient Church of the East.

---

[19] Acts 7:59-60; 12:1-2.
[20] Acts 9:1-2.
[21] Acts 15:5.

CHAPTER 15

GENTILES ENTERING THE KINGDOM

After this I will return and will build again the tabernacle of David which is fallen down; and I will build again the ruins thereof, and I will set it up: That the residue of men might seek after the Lord, and all the Gentiles, upon whom my name is called, saith the Lord, who doeth all these things. Acts 15: 16-17.

The Hebrew prophets had predicted that the Gentiles would participate in God's kingdom and reign. Both Amos and Isaiah recognized God's rule over the Gentile world. Isaiah prophesied that the Gentiles in Galilee would rejoice. He says that the people who dwelt in darkness (ignorance) would see a great light.[1] (Light in Semitic languages means "truth.")

The prophet Amos speaks about the Gentiles who are called by the name of God. These were to be invited into the kingdom, when the tabernacle of David would be mended and set up once more. Both the tabernacle and the kingdom were to be spiritual. The old tabernacle was symbolic of things to come.

The Jews were not to possess the Gentiles politically or materially, but spiritually. Jewish people were to share with them the truth of God by which they themselves had been blessed and set aside. "That they may possess the remnant of Edom and of all the heathen, which are called by my name, saith the Lord that doeth this."[2]

James quotes from Amos. He proves that God, from the very beginning, has been mindful of the Gentile nations. He also says that the Gentiles need not be compelled to observe certain Jewish laws which were enacted solely for the Jewish people at a time when they were living in the desert. It was the grace of God that saved the

---

[1] Isa. 9:1-2.
[2] Amos 9:12, K. J. V.

Gentiles, and therefore they were exempt from the observance of Jewish religious traditions.

STRANGLED

But that we write unto them, that they abstain from pollutions of idols, and from fornication, and from things strangled, and from blood.
Acts 15:20.

Jews were prohibited from eating the meat and the blood of strangled animals. Even touching an animal's dead body is considered unclean. The meat of sheep and cattle that are killed by a boulder or other accidental means is given to dogs.[3] These observances date back to the time of Moses. (Near Eastern Christians and Muslims still adhere to biblical ordinances concerning food and the eating of blood.)

Gentile followers of Jesus ate all kinds of meat. Jesus' Jewish disciples found it difficult to have any dealings with them. In the eyes of the Jews, Gentiles were unclean. At this time, Jewish Christians were in the majority and were in control of the Church. The apostles and missionaries were all of the Jewish faith; therefore, the observance of the Mosaic law was necessary. Gentiles were instructed to follow the apostolic ordinances so that they would not offend the Jewish followers of Jesus.[4]

Jesus observed the laws of the Jewish religion. As to the question of food, he told his disciples that what enters into a man cannot defile him; only the evil that comes out can defile him.[5] Nonetheless, the early disciples of Jesus, under the apostles, were required to observe some of the Jewish restrictions.

---

[3]Lev. 22:8.
[4]Rom 14:15.
[5]Mk. 7:15-23

BOOKS OF MOSES

For Moses of old time hath in every city them that preach him, being read in the synagogues every sabbath day. Acts 15:21.

Prior to the Babylonian captivity and the destruction of the temple in Jerusalem in 586 BCE, the books of Moses constituted the only sacred literature of the Hebrews. Most of the other books in the Bible had not yet been written; those which may have been written were not recognized as sacred. Priests were opposed to the prophets. Most of the latter were persecuted and put to death.

The five books of Moses—Genesis, Exodus, Leviticus, Numbers, and Deuteronomy—composed the Torah. These books contained laws and ordinances given to Moses when he was in the desert. Portions of Scripture were read on the Sabbath and sections of the scrolls were used in many parts of the country during national festivals. They were studied by priests and Levites and taught to the people.

Kings, judges and elders were to have the books that contained laws for judging the people. These scrolls were also read at gatherings. "And he took the book of the covenant and read in the audience of the people . . . ."[6] Mosaic code also demanded that the king must have a copy of the same law that was in the possession of the priests and Levites.[7]

The term "Moses" in this verse refers to the books of Moses. This does not imply that Moses wrote all of them but that they contain an account of his words and works. Moses' death and burial are recorded in some of them.

In the Near East, books are often called by the name of the person about whom they are written. The author or compiler does not always mention his own name. For example, according to this method of writing, a book written by Abraham Lincoln about George Washington would be entitled "Washington." Lincoln's name would

---

[6]Ex. 24:7.
[7]Dt. 17:15, 18-20.

not appear in it. Of course, it is believed by a few biblical scholars that Moses probably did write some of the laws and ordinances. He was well educated but he also employed scribes.[8]

The books of the prophets were adopted later and read in the synagogue. In the worship service the law was read first and the prophets afterward.[9]

WRITING

And they wrote letters by them after this manner; The apostles and elders and brethren send greeting unto the brethren which are of the Gentiles in Antioch and Syria and Cilicia. Acts 15:23.

This is the first evidence in Scripture that the apostles employed writing to keep in touch with churches about their teaching. In places where letter writing is not common and post offices unheard of, most messages are transmitted orally. In these cases, a message is usually dictated to a messenger who is to repeat it word for word. Only official documents and important church and government decrees are written. In some cases where professional writers are not available, people are informed of such decrees by word of mouth.

Writing was common in the holy land. The alphabet had been in use in Palestine from the eighth or ninth century BCE. In the time of the apostles, the entire Hebrew Scriptures were in written form. Commentaries on the Bible, teachings of great Jewish sages and traditions were also in writing. When a man divorced his wife, he gave her divorce papers, which had to be in writing.[10]

It is evident that the apostles had recorded all the teachings of

---

[8] Modern Old Testament scholars do not believe that Moses is responsible for the first five books. They also question whether Moses ever existed. This commentary does not involve itself in the modern approach to Scripture but with the Aramaic language and Near Eastern culture—that is, the customs and manners.

[9] Acts 13:15.

[10] See Mt. 5:31; 19:7; Mk. 10:4.

Jesus and most of their official business. Matthew's gospel was in circulation and in the possession of missionaries who were heralding the joyful message of God's kingdom. Like the Jewish authorities, the Christian movement had scribes who attended to the official business of the church. This is how Luke had access to events that had taken place years before his conversion.

A written official document would carry more weight among the Christians in Antioch than an oral message delivered by Paul. This would be especially so because a few years before this time Paul had been persecuting Jesus' disciples.

This apostolic epistle was written to Jewish and Syrian converts in their own language, Aramaic, which was also the language of the apostles and the official tongue of the church. Similar letters were written to other congregations. "And as they went through the cities, they delivered them the decrees for to keep, that were ordained of the apostles and elders which were in Jerusalem."[11]

The Gentile Christians were admonished to abstain from the eating of blood, the worship of idols, fornication and eating meat of strangled animals. These instructions were in accordance with Mosaic law. The Gentile converts were not aware of and did not observe these ordinances because they were never under the law of Moses. This created a disturbance among the Jewish converts who were strict followers of their religious laws. They could not understand how a Gentile could become a Christian without first pledging his loyalty to these Mosaic laws.

The apostles wanted to avoid a breach between the Jewish followers of Jesus and the Gentile Christians, so they ordered the latter to conform to the law of Moses. At that time, the Jewish Christians were in the majority. They believed that the teachings of Jesus were the fulfillment of Judaism.

The instructions were writen so that nothing could be added or omitted from what the Holy Spirit had revealed to the apostles. In the Near East, ordinances and laws pertaining to matters of faith are

---

[11]Acts 16:4, K. J. V.

delivered in writing. Even the Mosaic law was given in writing at a time when writing was very new. Unfortunately, the letters that the apostles had composed for the Christians in Antioch, Syria and Cilicia are lost. Luke touches only on the important points of the decrees. The other material that these letters contained are not mentioned.

KOSHER

That ye abstain from meats offered to idols, and from blood and from things strangled, and from fornication: from which if ye keep yourselves, ye shall do well. Fare ye well. Acts 15:29.

As stated above, the law of Moses prohibited the eating of blood and the flesh of animals strangled or torn by wild beasts.[12] To this day, Orthodox Jews eat only kosher meat—that is, meat approved by their religious authorities. The animal's head must be severed and the body left to bleed until every drop of blood is gone. Both Muslims and Near Eastern Christians still observe this biblical law. They do not eat the meat of an animal whose head is not severed. They also keep other Jewish religious ordinances relative to food.

The first Christians were adherents to the Jewish faith. Many of them were brought up strictly according to the law of Moses and the traditions of the elders. Jesus had revealed the inner meaning of the law and prophets but had not recommended a change in the law. He had come to fulfill the law and not to destroy it. This is the reason the apostles and their followers observed all of the Mosaic laws but rejected some of the traditions of the elders (the oral law).

The disciples in Antioch were asked to observe these laws to encourage the Jewish Christians and other Jews who might become disciples. They were told especially to abstain from eating the things offered to idols and from fornication.[13]

---

[12]Gen. 9:4; Lev. 22:8.
[13]See 1 Cor. 8:10.

Jesus' early disciples were required to maintain exemplary conduct so that they could carry on the work of spreading the gospel of the kingdom. Christians were to live in purity and sincerity so that their good works and behavior would be noticed by the Jews and pagans.

SYRIA

And he went through Syria and Cilicia, confirming the churches. Acts 15:41.

Syria is the name of the country west of the Euphrates river, between Palestine and Asia Minor. Tyre, Sidon and Beirut are the important seaports, serving Transjordan and parts of Arabia. The largest cities are Damascus (the capital), Antioch and Aleppo. Most of these cities are located on commercial routes between Europe and the Near East. The country used to be rather poor. For a living, its inhabitants depended on caravans and the transfer of merchandise through its ports.

During the time of Paul, Syria was a Roman province to which Palestine was subordinate. "And this taxing was first made when Cyrenius was governor of Syria."[14]

One must not confuse Syria with Assyria (Iraq), nor Syrians with Assyrians. The countries adjoin each other and their names are similar in English but not in Aramaic, which once was the language of both countries. In Aramaic, Assyria was called *Athor* and Syria was called *Sur* and *Aram*. The name of Syria is derived from the province of Suria, which the Greeks renamed Tyre. The city of Tyre was famed for its shipbuilding, trading and its dye works. Syrians were the builders of one of the greatest civilizations of the world. They had a large merchant marine and were accomplished in working steel, iron and brass.

Syria and Lebanon still have a large Christian population. The

---

[14] Lk. 2:2, K. J. V.

inhabitants of this region are Aramean in their origin and Maronites in religion. (The Maronites are a Christian sect under Rome.)

CHAPTER 16

TIMOTHEUS

Then came he to Derbe and Lystra: and, behold, a certain disciple was there, named Timotheus, the son of a certain woman which was a Jewess and believed; but his father was a Greek: Acts 16:1.

According to the Aramaic Peshitta text, Timothy's father was Aramean (Syrian) and his mother was Jewish. As Syria borders on Palestine, a great many Syrian men had married Jewish women. The children from such marriages were generally reared in the Jewish faith. Usually, these women won the favor of their husbands and succeeded in converting them to their religion. This was also true of Titus, whose father was Aramean and his mother Jewish.

At that time Syrian religions were dying out, so much so that many Syrians had become interested in the Jewish faith. They attended synagogue meetings and observed some of the Jewish customs but did not practice circumcision.

Many of these men were glad to accept Jesus' gospel of the kingdom in preference to Judaism. The reason for this is that the Jews demanded strict adherence to the Jewish traditions and racial customs.

Paul was preaching among the Jews and among the Gentiles who were interested in Jewish worship. He circumcised Timothy for fear of the strictness of the Jews. The Jews would not have permitted Paul to preach to them if he had kept, in his company, an Aramean who was not circumcised.

Timothy became a fervent preacher of the Jesus' gospel of the kingdom. He was also a faithful companion to Paul. Years later, Paul appointed him overseer (bishop) of the churches in Cyprus.

GUIDED BY THE SPIRIT

After they were come to Mysia, they assayed to go into Bithynia: but the Spirit suffered them not. Acts 16:7.

"The Spirit suffered them not" is an Aramaic expression which means that they were warned through a vision or a divine communication not to go into Bithynia.

Semites believe in dreams, visions and prophecies and ask holy men about them. Hebrew kings consulted their prophets before they went to war. King Saul consulted with the prophet, Samuel, when he fought against the Philistines. King Ahab sought the advice of the prophets when he wanted to declare war on Syria.[1]

Usually when faithful followers are warned about something by a man of God or by a vision, they obey. Paul was so sure that he was being guided by God's spirit that he postponed his departure. On other occasions, he received instructions through revelations and he complied immediately.[2] Those who rely on God are guided and directed.

WE AND THEY

And after he had seen the vision, immediately we endeavoured to get into Macedonia, assuredly gathering that the Lord had called us for to preach the gospel unto them. Acts 16:10.

The first person plural "we" is used to include Luke, the author of the book of Acts. He accompanied Paul to Macedonia. When the writer is with Paul, he uses "we." It is evident from the style of the book of Acts that Luke performed the task of a reporter.

On some occasions, Luke was not present with Paul. Persecutions, expenses and emergencies made it impossible for Paul to have

---

[1] 1 Ki. 22:6-7.
[2] Acts 16:9-10 and Gal. 2:2.

all of his co-workers with him. It also seems reasonable to suppose that Paul left some of his co-workers behind to take care of the new disciples and take charge of the work that they had begun. At times, he sent some of them to visit congregations and look after important matters for him.

In this instance, Paul's departure was rather sudden. He was told in a vision to go to Macedonia.[3] When the author was not with Paul, he relied on the information that Paul and his other companions passed on to him. Luke was very modest; he kept himself in the background when reporting the events he had witnessed.

Paul, like other Near Eastern Semites, believed in visions and was guided by them. He even foresaw the difficulties and the imprisonment he would endure at Jerusalem.[4] Peter also was sent on an important mission to Caesarea through a vision that came to him at Joppa.[5]

SHRINES

And from thence to Philippi, which is the chief city of that part of Macedonia, and a colony: and we were in that city abiding certain days. And on the sabbath we went out of the city by a river side, where prayer was wont to be made: and we sat down and spake unto the women which resorted thither. Acts 16:12-13.

The Aramaic text reads: "And from thence to Philippi, which is the capital of Macedonia, and is a colony; and we were in that city on certain holidays. And on the sabbath day we went outside the city gate to the riverside because a house of prayer was seen there, and when we were seated, we spoke to the women who had gathered there."[6]

---

[3] 2 Cor. 2:13.
[4] See Acts 21:11.
[5] Acts 10:17-23.
[6] Acts 16:12-13, Aramaic Peshitta text, Lamsa translation.

In the ancient days, temples, shrines and houses of prayer were erected outside the city walls, a long distance from business sites, bathing houses and other public places. In the Near East, places of worship are in a special location, and people believe that the ground around them is sacred. Today one finds ancient churches and shrines outside the towns and cities. Some of them are from half a mile to two miles away; others are even farther. People visit these shrines for prayer.

"A house of prayer" does not necessarily mean that this was a church with chairs, lamps, books and a custodian. Today, most of these "houses of prayer" are desolate places. Some of them are ancient abandoned churches, but the ruins are still venerated. Others are small shrines with four walls and a small door; some of them have roofs and others are uncovered.

For example, the Kurdish people have no churches and generally worship at such places. They call them *Misgaud*—that is, "the place of worship." Some of these shrines are near streams and brooks because Near Easterners wash their hands before they enter a shrine or church to pray. Muslims wash both their hands and feet.

It seems that there was no Jewish synagogue at Philippi. The Jews went outside the city to pray in the out-of-doors, as people still do, in the towns where churches, mosques and synagogues are not to be found. This is true especially of small groups that cannot afford to build a place of worship. They pray in houses, ruins of ancient temples, abandoned shrines and, at times, in the open. Each person prays alone, sometimes kneeling, sometimes standing.

During holidays, the shrines and places of prayer are visited by a great many people. Some come to worship, others to meet friends, and still others come out of curiosity. Vendors also seek buyers for their dry-goods, food, perfume and other merchandise. These places serve as common grounds until the sun goes down; they are deserted until the next holiday.

This was a Jewish holy day, the Sabbath. Jewish worshipers ceased all kinds of work and spent their time leisurely walking or going to places of prayer.

WOMAN MERCHANT CONVERTED

And when she was baptized and her household, she besought us, saying, If ye have judged me to be faithful to the Lord, come into my house, and abide there. And she constrained us. Acts 16:15.

The Aramaic text reads: "And a certain woman, named Lydia, a seller of purple of the city of Thyatira, feared God; her heart was so touched by our Lord that she listened to what Paul said. And she was baptized together with her household, and she begged us, saying, If you are sincerely convinced that I believe in our Lord, come and stay in my house; and she urged us strongly."[7]

Businessmen and merchants are not readily trusted. The reason is that business is carried on by bargaining, taking of oaths, and lying, so that what a merchant says is not always taken seriously. In addition, merchants generally do not quarrel over religion and theology while they are bargaining with a prospective customer. Both merchant and buyer agree on many disputed and hair-splitting doctrines until the deal is terminated. Some salesmen would not hesitate in pretending to be of the same faith as the buyer. When the bargaining fails, the customer and merchant reveal their true faith and then curse each other's religion.

Lydia was a small silk merchant or a peddler. She was not quite convinced that Paul believed her to be a sincere person. To prove that she had accepted his message, she invited Paul and his companions to her home to break bread with her and the household. This is one of the strongest proofs that any Near Easterner can offer to evince genuine sincerity. Usually members of one faith never have social dealings with those of another faith.

Lydia wanted to demonstrate her pure and absolute faith in Jesus' gospel of the kingdom through her hospitality. Paul and his companions were strangers in the city and needed a place to lodge. This was the perfect way to show them that she was truly sincere. She began to "urge" or "constrain" them to accept her hospitality in

---

[7]Acts 16:14-16, Aramaic Peshitta text, Lamsa translation.

typical Near Eastern manners.

According to Dr. Abraham M. Rihbany, when one extends such hospitality in genuine Eastern fashion, it is no small matter. "Semitic effusiveness and intensity of speech are never more strenuously exercised than on such occasions." He further says:

> Brevity on such occasions is the soul of stinginess. The brief form of the American invitation, "I should be pleased to have you dine with us, if you can," however sincere, would seem to an Oriental [Near Easterner] like an excuse to escape the obligation of hospitality. Again, the ready acceptance of an invitation in the West would seem to the son of the East utterly undignified. Although the would-be guest could accept, he must be as insistent in saying, "No, I can't," as the would-be host in saying, "Yes, you must."
>
> Approaching his hoped-for guest, a Syrian engages him in something like the following dialogue, characterized by a glow of feeling which the translation can only faintly reveal:
>
> "Ennoble us by your presence."
> "I would be ennobled but I cannot accept."
> "That cannot be."
> "Yea, yea, it must be."
> "No, I swear against you by our friendship and by the life of God. I love just to acquaint you with my bread and salt."
> "I swear also that I find it impossible to accept. Your bread and salt are known to all."
> "Yea, to do it just for our good. By coming to us you come to your own home. Let us repay your bounty to us."
> "By the mercy of God, I have not bestowed any bounty upon you worth mentioning."

Here the host seizes his guest by the arm and with an emphatic, "I will not let you," pulls at him and would drag him bodily into his house. Then the guest, happy in being vanquished "with honor," consents to the invitation.[8]

PAUL ENCOUNTERS A SOOTHSAYER

And it came to pass as we went to prayer, a certain damsel possessed with a spirit of divination met us, which brought her masters much gain by soothsaying: The same followed Paul and us, and cried, saying, These men are the servants of the most high God, which shew unto us the way of salvation. And this did she many days. But Paul being grieved, turned and said to the spirit, I command thee in the name of Jesus Christ to come out of her. And he came out the same hour. Acts 16:16-18.

Part 1—SOOTHSAYING. The Aramaic word *kisma*, "soothsaying" or "fortune-telling," derives from *kasam*, "to deliver an oracle." A *kasoma* is the deliverer of messages and interpreter of past and future events. This type of medium is similar to a Near Eastern astrologer who tries tracing the causes of illness, accidents and other misfortunes and prescribes remedies.

Stars and so-called "unseen spirits" are blamed for all misfortunes. Soothsayers are the sole authorities in this field because no one can examine the stars or converse with spirits to verify facts. Therefore, they are never challenged nor disputed by those who seek their aid and follow their advice.

In the Near East some soothsayers diagnose cases by opening an old manuscript that contains many complicated formulas. The consultant puts his hand on a certain letter referring to a certain passage in the book. This passage describes the cause of an illness and also prescribes a remedy. Such documents are very rare and jealously guarded.

Another form of fortune-telling is called *zakoreh*. In this case the medium goes into a trance and attempts to communicate with the spirits of the departed. Some of the soothsayers use a small copper or

---

[8]Abraham M. Rihbany, *The Syrian Christ,* Chapter Three, "Compel them to Come in," pp. 208-209.

silver bowl that they fill with water before they begin to converse with the spirits. Then the medium claims to describe the person with whom there is a communication.

Fortune-telling is a prosperous vocation. Students of the art become rich quickly. Large sums of money are paid by the credulous public. Even governors, princes and kings become ardent followers of these men and women. (Read the story of the woman of Endor who claimed to converse with the spirit of Samuel.[9])

When a medium is a woman, a male guardian always attends her. In the Near East, it is not considered proper for a strange man to be in the presence of a female medium. The guardian or protector will deliver the message for her. A male guardian also becomes the master of the fortune-teller.

Sometimes a male who seeks a reading or consultation with a female medium will disguise himself in women's clothing so that he may freely enter the medium's home without the guardian being present. But he is very likely to be detected by the psychic reader. King Saul did this very thing when he consulted with the woman of Endor who was experienced in conversing with the departed. But she recognized him at once.[10]

Most of these women are unmarried and free to be hired by men who take them to cities where their practice is profitable and where there is no competition. In Paul's day, female mediums were often bought and sold. The owners of this medium probably paid a large sum for her and expected good returns from her work. When Paul stopped her from crying out about them and freed her from the powers that dominated her, her masters' hopes were shattered. They took immediate action against Paul because he ruined their business.

Part 2—A MEDIUM. The word "spirit" here refers to the power that enables the medium to see into the present dilemma and make predictions of its outcome. In other words, the term "spirit" refers to the power that motivates divining and fortune-telling. There are many

---

[9] 1 Sam. 28:7-14.
[10] 1 Sam. 28:8, 12.

such individuals in the Near East who claim to possess mysterious powers that can tell future events, advise, heal and practice certain magic. Usually people in distress consult them.

During ancient times when biblical Israel had only judges to guide the nation, men and women "with familiar spirits" (mediums) were numerous. Samuel sought to exterminate them. King Saul sought help from the woman of Endor.

A person who has a "familiar spirit" is a sort of mystic. The work is done by deep concentration. After a long period of chanting and intense mental effort, the medium will describe the person with whom contact is desired and delivers a message. The mystified inquirer may also see a mental image of that person.

This girl recognized that Paul was endowed with powers superior to her own. In observing and studying him, she quickly learned how wrong she had been. She then realized that her power was not real and permanent. Therefore, she followed Paul and sought his help to free her. She was probably ashamed of her practice of divining.

Paul rebuked the "spirit"—that is, the enabling power in her. She became normal and free of the practice. The moment she was healed, it severed the relationship with her masters This act displeased these owners, so they immediately seized Paul and Silas. They brought them before the court and had them beaten. But truth and justice cannot be stopped. Just as the rays of the sun cause snow to melt, so does the light of truth destroy error and unjust paths.

STRIPPED

And the multitude rose up together against them: and the magistrates rent off their clothes, and commanded to beat them. Acts 16:22.

The Aramaic text reads: "And a large crowd gathered against them. Then the soldiers stripped them of their clothes and gave command to scourge them."[11] Scourging is still common in many parts of the Near East, especially among primitive people. The prisoners are stripped of their outer garments, laid on the ground, then beaten by two men who stand on each side of the condemned. In some cases, all the clothes are removed and the victims are continually whipped until they are unconscious.

According to the Aramaic text, Paul and Silas were brought before the soldiers and the city officials, who accused them of preaching and teaching customs alien to those of that region. (The soldiers were Romans, but the officials were natives.)

They were charged with having incited the crowds. Then the soldiers stripped Paul and Silas of their clothes and ordered them to be whipped. The city was under the Roman authorities. Native officials and judges had jurisdiction in local matters only. Paul and Silas were strangers from countries that were also under Roman rule.

ROMAN CITIZENS

But Paul said unto them, They have beaten us openly uncondemned, being Romans, and have cast us into prison; and now do they thrust us out privily? Nay verily; but let them come themselves and fetch us out.
Acts 16:37.

The Aramaic text reads: "But Paul said to him, Not having committed any offense, they flogged us, Roman citizens, in the presence of the people, and they cast us into prison; and now do they let us out secretly? No verily: let them come themselves and take us out."[12]

The term "Romans" means "Roman citizens" and not merely natives of Rome or other parts of Italy. Paul was a Hebrew of the tribe of Benjamin, a Jew by religion and a Roman citizen by nationality. He was born in Tarsus, a city in Cilicia, not far from

---

[11]Acts 16:22, Aramaic Peshitta text, Lamsa translation.
[12]Acts 16:37, Aramaic Peshitta text, Lamsa translation.

Syria. This part of Asia Minor was made a Roman province. Hence, its citizens were considered Romans.

Other regions such as Palestine, Transjordan and some areas of Syria, were ruled by Roman emperors or the Senate. Since the inhabitants of these countries had some kind of home rule, they were subject to the laws of their land. Roman citizens, on the other hand, were treated with high respect and with utmost care. When charged with crimes they were tried before Roman officials. At this time, Roman citizens had extraterritorial rights.

(This was true of British citizens in Egypt, Iraq, Transjordan and Palestine. An English subject in these countries could not be tried or punished by a native court. He was tried by a British tribunal or consul. These countries had been mandated by Britain. Therefore, British officials and military authorities could arrest, try and punish natives, but they usually had to refer a case to the native court with whom they acted jointly.)

CHAPTER 17

PAUL PREACHES IN THE SYNAGOGUE

Opening and alleging, that Christ must needs have suffered, and risen again from the dead; and that this Jesus, whom I preach unto you, is Christ. And some of them believed, and consorted with Paul and Silas; and of the devout Greeks a great multitude, and of the chief women not a few.
Acts 17:3-4.

The Aramaic text reads: "Then they passed by the cities of Amphipolis and Apollonia, and came to Thessalonica, where there was a synagogue of the Jews. And Paul, as was his custom, went in to join them, and for three sabbaths he spoke to them from the scriptures, interpreting and proving that Christ [Messiah] had to suffer and rise again from the dead; and that he is the same Jesus Christ whom I preach to you. And some of them believed and joined Paul and Silas; and many of them were Greeks who revered God, and many of them were well known women, a goodly number."[1]

Part 1—THE MESSIAH/CHRIST MUST SUFFER. Paul confirms what Jesus had said concerning his suffering, death and resurrection. Jesus, prior to his ordeal and crucifixion, had told his disciples many times that he would be crucified and that he would rise again. "Saying that the Son of man had to be delivered into the hands of sinful men, and be crucified, and rise again on the third day."[2]

Even after his resurrection, he told some of his disciples that they should have known that the Messiah/Christ was to suffer and that Scripture that predicted his death must be fulfilled. "Then he said to them, O fools, and slow of heart to believe all that the prophets have spoken: ought not Christ to have suffered these things, and to

---

[1] Acts 17:1-4, Aramaic Peshitta text, Lamsa translation.
[2] Lk. 24:7, Aramaic Peshitta text, Lamsa translation.

enter into his glory?"³

The Jews were expecting the coming of a Messiah who would restore the kingdom of David and establish a political rule over the world. Paul was avowing that there is no other Savior coming and that Jesus of Nazareth is the promised Messiah who had to suffer and rise in glory.

In was difficult for the Jewish people to reconcile the idea of a conquering Messiah predicted by the early Hebrew prophets with a God-anointed leader who died on a cross. To them, the promised one was to be the messenger of God empowered to rule throughout the world and live forever. They did not deny the miracles and wonders that Jesus had done nor his powerful teaching for peace, but they could *not* believe in a crucified, defeated Messiah. Their promised leader was to be an everlasting ruler who would restore Israel to its former glory and, more than likely, even greater glory.

Part 2—GREEK CONVERTS. This is one of the few references to Greek people in the New Testament that is also found in the Aramaic Peshitta text. The Aramaic word for "Greeks" is *Yonayeh*. In many other passages, the term "Greeks" in New Testament English translations is based on Greek versions of scripture. This is why there are so many references to "Greeks" in our English versions. But in the Aramaic Peshitta text, the word *Aramayeh*, meaning "Arameans" or "Syrians," is present and not "Greeks." Translators, for some unknown reason, changed the word *Aramayeh* to the Greek word *Helenos*, "Greeks."

It is true that Greeks in Asia Minor, Macedonia and Greece were among the first converts to Christianity. They inhabited countries bordering on Syria. Greeks are closer to Semitic peoples than any European races. Some of their customs and manners are very similar. Greeks are hospitable and religiously inclined. Much of their alphabet is based on the Aramaic alphabet.

These early Greek disciples were somewhat influenced by Hebrew thought. The Hebrews believed in one God and despised

---

³Lk. 24:25-26, K. J. V.

image worship. Greeks were great thinkers and were easily convinced that their idols were not the work of the divine spirit but the works of men. Some of the Greeks had joined the Jewish synagogues. They worshiped the God of heaven and were devout in every respect.

IDOL WORSHIP

Now while Paul waited for them at Athens, his spirit was stirred in him, when he saw the city wholly given to idolatry. Acts 17:16.

Jewish law prohibited idolatry. Moses decreed that the worship and veneration of images or any other man-made objects is a transgression. No God was to be worshiped except Yahweh, the God of Israel, the living God.[4]

Hebrew prophets from Moses to Elijah were against the practice of worshiping idols. In those days, this type of veneration was known as "Baal worship." Most of the books in the Hebrew Bible condemn the making and adoration of these images. Nonetheless, from time to time, Hebrew people reverted to idol worship and for many centuries continued to do so until it was eventually destroyed. Scripture refers to idols as deaf and dumb gods, who had ears but could not hear, eyes but could not see, and mouths but could not speak. "For all the gods of the nations are idols: but the Lord made the heavens."[5] In the New Testament, this kind of adoration was called "devil[6] worship" because it was crazy to worship an idol made of stone or gold.

Greeks, like other pagans, worshiped images whose deities were mysterious and capricious. They also worshiped idols of kings and great heroes. Paul was a strict follower of the Jewish faith but had been converted to Jesus' teaching and had become a preacher of his gospel of the kingdom. "His spirit stirred in him" means Paul was displeased by the sight of so many images and the manner in which

---

[4] Ex. 20:1-5.
[5] Ps. 96:5.
[6] The word "devil" in Aramaic means "crazy."

these idols were venerated.

Paul had changed his mind about some of the Jewish traditions that he was taught concerning ceremonies and customs, but he still revered and obeyed the basic commandments. The scene at Athens displayed a flagrant violation of the first and second commandments. Therefore, Paul was provoked in his spirit to see these Greeks and their philosophers worshiping the work of their own hands.

A human being is a child of God and therefore the likeness of God. In Paul's mind, humans should not bow to things that were created for humankind. "Now therefore man, being of the family of God, is not bound to worship resemblances made of gold or silver or stone shaped by the skill and knowledge of man into resemblances of Deity."[7]

AREOPAGUS

(For all the Athenians and strangers which were there spent their time in nothing else, but either to tell, or to hear some new thing.) Acts 17:21.

Areopagus was a large courthouse with several courtyards and halls. Idle persons and strangers to Athens often gathered outside the court to hear philosophers expound their theories and orators deliver addresses and debate on subjects of current interest. Areopagus was something like Hyde Park in London or Columbus Circle in New York.

According to the Aramaic text, Paul was arrested or compelled to go to the court at the Areopagus. He would have to explain his teachings, which were alien and disturbing to the Greeks. Paul succeeded in converting a number of the people. Among these new followers was Dionysius, one of the judges of the Areopagus. Other listeners mocked Paul; the rest were indifferent.

---

[7]Acts 17:29, Aramaic Peshitta text, Lamsa translation.

PAUL ADDRESSES THE ATHENIANS

Then Paul stood in the midst of Mar's hill, and said, Ye men of Athens, I perceive that in all things ye are too superstitious. For as I passed by, and beheld your devotions. I found an altar with the inscriptions TO THE UNKNOWN GOD. Whom therefore ye ignorantly worship, him declare I unto you. God that made the world and all things therein, seeing that he is Lord of heaven and earth, dwelleth not in temples made with hands; Neither is worshipped with men's hands, as though he needed any thing, seeing he giveth to all life and breath, and all things; And hath made of one blood all nations of men for to dwell on all the face of the earth, and hath determined the times before appointed, and the bounds of their habitation; That they should seek the Lord, if haply they might feel after him, and find him, though he be not far from every one of us: For in him we live, and move, and have our being; as certain also of your own poets have said, For we are also his offspring. Acts 17: 22-28.

Part 1—WORSHIPING IMAGES. Verse 22 of the Aramaic text reads: "When Paul stood in the court at Areopagus, he said, Men of Athens, I see that above all things you are extravagant in the worship of idols." *Deglat shedeh* in Aramaic refers to image worship and its ritual. Pagan peoples venerated statues and images with pomp and ceremony, including the burning of candles and incense. The idols were at the center of the highly organized pagan worship.

Shedeh in Aramaic means "demons, devils, insane things." These images and idols were not real, and worshiping them was insanity in the sight of the Jews. Hebrew prophets denounced idols and referred to them as devilish (crazy), deaf and dumb.[8]

According to the Aramaic text, Paul told the Athenians that they were *yateereen*, "rich, excellent," implying "extravagant" in their image worship and its ritual. He had seen many idols that had been donated by worshipers.

In the Near East, no one would attempt to reproach, in the slightest degree, the worship or the sacred shrines of the adherents of a rival faith, especially at the very site itself. Such an act would lead

---

[8]See also Ps. 115:4-8.

to quarrels and bloodshed. No matter how much Semites may disagree on their theology and religion, when visiting other churches and shrines they will usually make compliments about the building, the images and the ritual. For example, a Muslim will praise a Christian image in a church if he happens to be present on some state occasion, although in his heart he may curse it and ask God's forgiveness for having even looked at such a deplorable object.

Paul was not interested in Greek worship and its ritual. His casual complimentary remarks were intended as bait so that he could win the good will and interest of the Greeks. Semitic missionaries always try to gain the confidence of the people among whom they are working by stressing something they all have in common. Like Jesus, Paul disregarded the established Jewish customs and was friendly toward pagans. What concerned him most was how to bring them to Jesus' teaching.

Part 2—PAGAN SANCTUARY. Verse 23 in Aramaic reads: "For as I walked about, and viewed the house of your idols [a sanctuary], I found an altar with this inscription: *THIS IS THE ALTAR OF THE UNKNOWN GOD*. He therefore, while you know him not but yet worship him, is the very one I am preaching to you."[9] The Aramaic phrase *beth dhlatkhon,* means "sanctuary" (literally "house of your idols").

In Christian churches, the altar is used for communion. In Assyrian churches, altars are situated in the sanctuaries, the most holy place in the sacred building. In ancient days, sanctuaries and images were generally built through the generosity and gifts of the rich and noble. Idols were donated by tribes as memorials in the temples for tribal patron saints, around whom the clan's history and traditions were centered.

People visited sanctuaries during feast days, bringing costly gifts, foods and animal sacrifices. This custom still prevails among some Christians and Muslims in remote areas of the Near East who patronize and care for certain sanctuaries, graves of saints and other

---

[9]Acts 17:23, Aramaic Peshitta text, Lamsa translation.

ancient shrines.

When a tribe was destroyed, its idols were either thrown out or incorporated into the faith of the conquering tribe under a different name. Consequently, the worship of these idols was neglected and their tradition forgotten. In due time, these abandoned shrines, bereft of worshipers and supporters, became lost in obscurity.

The altar to which Paul called attention was one of the oldest shrines and objects in the temple. Its name and tradition had been forgotten. The inscription, "The sanctuary of the unknown god," had been made in recent years. The other shrines and images still bore the original inscriptions containing the names of the donors. The worshipers were thus advised concerning their history and traditions.

Paul made reference to this mysterious sanctuary so that he might explain better his God, who also was not known and whose nature was a mystery to pagans accustomed to worshiping idols. Pagan cults in Greece had been imported from Babylon, Persia, and Egypt and were in their infancy.

Yahweh, the Hebrew God, was also worshiped by means of images and statues in the beginning. Abraham's father is said to have destroyed the images that had caused so much dispute and trouble in his country, and in so doing he discovered the true God. Mohammed likewise, after his victory over pagan Arabia, destroyed several hundred tribal idols (gods) at Mecca. In those ancient days, gods were responsible for many quarrels. Their respective worshipers disagreed and fought one another on their account.

Part 3—RACIAL EQUALITY. In verse 26, the Aramaic text reads: "And he [God] made of one blood all nations of men to dwell on all the face of the earth, and he has appointed seasons by his command, and has set limits to the age of men." The latter part of the verse is a quotation from the book of Psalms.

Paul explains to the men of Athens the universality of God, the sole creator and ruler of heaven and earth. It was God who had made of one blood all nations on the face of the earth.

The Hebrews believed in one God, maker of heaven and earth and everything that exists. "The heavens declare the glory of God;

and the firmament sheweth his handiwork."[10] Holy Scripture does reveal that God was just as interested in the Gentiles as in Israel. The Greeks, on the other hand, were idolaters. They believed in many gods with diverse interests. The god of one race had nothing to do with people of other races or tribes.

The doctrine of polytheism had been upheld by the Hebrews prior to the eighth century BCE. Although they believed in their God, Yahweh, they also believed in the existence of the Gentile gods. Of course, they understood Yahweh was supreme. Abraham believed in his God, but he did not deny the existence of other gods. This kind of belief is called henotheism. The Hebrew concept of pure monotheism crystallized later.

Semitic people believe in predestination; that is, they maintain that every event is ordained by God and that a man's life is governed and guided by the divine presence. However, they believe that human beings are endowed with free will to distinguish between right and wrong and can choose to follow the true path of life. They also hold to the belief that God knows what is in a person's heart and does not interfere with the free will of that individual.

Part 4—THE MEANING OF "IN HIM." "For in him we live and move and have our being, as some of your own wise men have said, For we are his kindred."[11] In this passage, the Aramaic word *Beh* means not just "in him" but "by him." Aramaic speaking people often say, "He does these things by the command of the king," or, "The governor stands by him," that is, supports him. The term "in him" literally means "by him," denoting "by God's grace, power, method." The first part of the verse may be translated as, "For through him we live and move, and have our being. . ."

Through the teaching of Jesus we learn that we are children of the living God. Our origin is God, who created us in his very image and likeness. This idea of spiritual sonship had become lost—that is, dormant—in the hearts of humanity, but Jesus restored this truth.

---

[10] Ps. 19:1 K. J. V.
[11] Acts 17:28, Aramaic Peshitta text, Lamsa translation.

Thus, through him or by means of him, we call God our Father, our Beloved, and all of us become one family in spirit and by this truth.

CHAPTER 18

SADDLEMAKERS

And because he was of the same craft, he abode with them, and wrought: for by their occupation they were tentmakers. Acts 18:3.

The Aramaic more accurately reads *lawlareh,* "saddlemakers," and not "tentmakers" as translated in the King James Version of the book of Acts.

Saddlemaking is an art in the Near East. Saddles always were, and still are, made by highly skilled artisans of this special trade. Boys from the age of ten or even younger are employed as apprentices. Some boys begin learning this specialized field of art from four to five years of age.

In Arabia and Palestine, tentmaking was never an art nor a business. Tents are never made for sale. These tents are made from the hair of goats and the material is spun and woven by women. Each family makes its own tents and repairs them as they wear out. But saddlemaking is usually done by men. Women make the embroidered cloth on the saddle and a few minor parts. Skilled male artisans work on the designs for the embroidered work and leather parts.

Saddles are still sold and bought in marketplaces and the saddlemaking industry is a thriving business, especially in large cities. The townspeople buy their saddles in these markets and expert artisans travel to far-off places where saddlemakers are not available. They make specially designed saddles for the chiefs of tribes. The trade as a whole is very prosperous.

Paul had learned this trade as a major means for making a living. In the Near East, scribes and doctors of religion, in order to earn a livelihood, often work as saddlemakers, coppersmiths, engravers, silversmiths or shoemakers. These trades are considered honorable occupations, from which educated and religious people do very well.

Missionaries and religious men of the Near East have always

supported themselves by the work of their hands. Salaries were unknown until this idea was introduced by Western missionaries. The unpaid missionaries work from eight to ten hours, and whenever they can, they lecture in the afternoons and nights. They have to teach when working people are at leisure.

Jesus did most of his preaching and healing during the evening hours because the people were working in the fields during the day. But he addressed the artisans and shopkeepers while they were at work in the marketplace. This custom prevails even at the present time in many areas of the Near East. Muslim religious men and missionaries preach in the markets where artisans and businessmen are engaged in their work.

Paul worked very diligently at his trade so that he might not burden the Christian disciples financially. In those early days, Christian teaching, almost everywhere, met with strong opposition and most of the disciples were poor. Paul, under no obligation to anyone, could be bold in his teaching and admonitions.

PAUL CHANGES HIS MISSIONARY COURSE

And when Silas and Timotheus were come from Macedonia, Paul was pressed in the spirit, and testified to the Jews that Jesus was Christ. And when they opposed themselves, and blasphemed, he shook his raiment, and said unto them, Your blood be upon your own heads; I am clean: from henceforth I will go unto the Gentiles. And he departed thence, and entered into a certain man's house, named Justus, one that worshipped God, whose house joined hard to the synagogue. Acts 18:5-7.

Part 1—PAUL OPPOSED. Verse 5 in Aramaic reads: "And when Silas and Timotheus came from Macedonia, Paul felt he was not free to speak, because the Jews opposed him and blasphemed as he testified that Jesus is the Christ [Messiah]."[1] The Aramaic word *aliss* means "pressed" or "suppressed."

---

[1] Acts 18:5, Aramaic Peshitta text, Lamsa translation.

Adverse circumstances were hindering Paul from preaching to the Jews. He was very eager to teach them, but many of the leaders cursed and did everything possible to interfere with his preaching.

Up until this time, Jewish leadership had been friendly to Paul and his companions. In every city where there was a Jewish synagogue they had asked Paul to speak to them. But now the religious authorities caught on to what Paul was doing. They received warning from Judea and other places that Paul had left Judaism and that he was converting Jewish people to Jesus' gospel.

At the beginning of Paul's mission, most of the Jews in Asia Minor and Greece were ignorant of the things that had taken place in Palestine. There were also some Jewish people and authorities who were indifferent to what happened in Judea. Now, however, the authorities were determined to do away with Paul. They sent their agents to the cities where he went and rallied the people against him and his mission.[2]

Part 2—SHAKING ONE'S CLOTHES. Verse 6 in Aramaic reads: "So he shook his garments and said to them, From henceforth I am not to be blamed for what I am about to do; I am going to the Gentiles."[3] "Shaking one's raiment" and throwing dust and ashes on one's head is a common custom among Near Easterners.

When men wish to renounce or repudiate certain people or ideas and actions, they shake off the outer robe from the front. This means they are through or they have had it. This custom is similar to the shaking of dust from the sandals. Also, some men take a little dirt from the ground or a stone and throw it away, saying "I have no part with this." Where there are no sandals nor stones to be found, people shake the dust off their outer garments. They are physically demonstrating that they will have nothing further to do with the matter in question. Today, we say, "I wash my hand of it," as Pilate did.

Until now, Paul had obeyed the command of his Lord and the apostles. From the outset, he preached first to the Jews. But when he

---

[2]Acts 17:13; 18:12.
[3]Acts 18:6, Aramaic Peshitta text, Lamsa translation.

saw that the Jewish authorities and many of the people were balking and resisting his preaching, he changed his strategy and told them he would now preach to the Gentiles. He would go among the Arameans, Greeks and Romans.

Paul had been sincerely seeking the Jews and the descendants of the Ten Tribes, preaching to them in their synagogues and in the homes of the converts. Even as a prisoner in Rome, he first preached to the Jews. Paul was zealous to help his people to understand and accept the truth of Jesus' gospel. And like Jesus, he sought his own first, but now they were rejecting him.

Part 3—TITUS NOT JUSTUS. Verse 7 in Aramaic reads: "And he departed thence and entered into the house of a certain man named Titus, a devout man whose household had joined the synagogue."[4] The name "Justus" is not mentioned in the Aramaic text.

Missionaries and travelers always seek lodging in the homes of their fellow-workers and converts. On their arrival in a town they inquire about other followers of their faith, and if there are none to be found, they lodge in a *khan* (an inn). This is true of missionaries who are not welcome in places where the feeling between believers of rival faiths is bitter.

The phrase in the King James Version of verse 7, "whose house joined hard to the synagogue," is somewhat misleading. Generally, churches, synagogues and mosques are built at some distance from other buildings and dwellings and are surrounded by a courtyard about twenty to thirty feet out from the walls. This courtyard is enclosed by a stone or mud fence, thus setting the place apart from the rest of the town. Both the building and courtyard are considered sacred and no animals are allowed to enter. Muslims even forbid unbelievers to trespass on the sacred grounds. Christians often use the grounds for burial of holy men.

The Aramaic term *beteh* refers to his "household" or his "family." *Benibeteh* means "the members of his family or household." People often say to each other, *"Beti*, you are my house,"

---

[4] Acts 18:7, Aramaic Peshitta text, Lamsa translation.

meaning "you are a member of my family." Thus, the verse is to be understood as that Titus' family had joined the synagogue.

Titus' father was Aramean and his mother was Jewish. He was a member of the Jewish synagogue, but later Titus accepted Jesus' gospel of the kingdom. Hotels and public lodging places were scarce in those days. Travelers and missionaries were entertained by friends and converts, just as they are today. Titus accompanied Paul on his last journey to Jerusalem.[5] Paul mentions him in his other epistles.

A VOW

And Paul after this tarried there yet a good while, and then took his leave of the brethren, and sailed thence into Syria, and with him Priscilla and Aquila; having shorn his head in Cenchrea: for he had a vow. Acts 18:18.

Making vows is an ancient Semitic custom that is still practiced in Bible lands. A vow is a pledge to serve God, make an offering and give alms to the poor. It is a sign of thanksgiving for God's compassion and favors.

Often when an individual is to go on a long and hazardous journey or is to undertake a challenging and difficult task, he will make a vow. On the return from a journey, this person will offer a gift at a shrine. He may also have a sheep slaughtered and then distribute its meat among the people.

When Jacob fled from Esau, he made a vow to God in which he pledged a tenth of all that God would give him. "And Jacob vowed a vow, saying, If God will be with me and will keep me in this way that I go. . . . so that I come again to my father's house in peace; then shall the Lord be my God . . . and all that thou shalt give me I will surely give the tenth unto thee."[6]

Men or women who were dedicated to God often took vows that

---

[5]Gal. 2:2-3.
[6]Gen. 28:20-22, K. J. V.

they were not to touch a dead person. They would not drink wine or eat moist or dried grapes. Men would not shave their heads until the days of the vow had been fulfilled. Such were the biblical laws governing the Nazarites.[7] When the vow was over, a Nazarite was to shave his head (cut his hair) at the door of the tabernacle of the congregation. The hair would then be thrown into a fire.[8]

When Samson was conceived, the angel of the Lord told his mother not to drink wine or eat unclean things.[9] Samson let his hair grow long and was known as a Nazarite. (The long, uncut hair of a man who had taken a vow served as a reminder of the vow and the divine promises.) When Samson's hair was cut, he lost his strength. His power was not in the hair itself but in the divine promises that the long hair symbolized. Samson did not follow the instructions given to his mother by the angel of the Lord. He made his vow, but when he broke it, he lost both his faith and great might.

Women usually make vows when they have prayed for a male child. For example, the mother of the prophet Samuel had prayed for a male child. She vowed that she would give the child to the Lord.[10] Therefore, after Samuel was born, she gave him to the high priest, whose name was Eli.

Evidently, Paul had made a vow. He had not cut his hair for a certain period of time. When the days of the vow were fulfilled, he shaved his head while he was in Cenchrea. Now he was on his way to Jerusalem to attend the feast as was his custom.[11]

God had helped and guided him in every way. God had saved him from his enemies. His preaching mission had been fruitful. Upon his arrival at Jerusalem, Paul went to the temple with other men who, like himself, had taken vows.[12]

---

[7]Num. 6:2-20.
[8]Num. 6:18.
[9]Judges 13:7.
[10]1 Sam. 1:11.
[11]Acts 18:21.
[12]Acts 21:23-26.

FOLLOWERS OF JOHN THE BAPTIST

This man was instructed in the way of the Lord; and being fervent in the spirit, he spake and taught diligently the things of the Lord, knowing only the baptism of John. Acts 18:25.

The Aramaic text reads: "He had been converted to the way of the Lord, and was fervent in the spirit; he spoke and taught very fully concerning Jesus, but he knew only the baptism of John."[13] *Mariah* is the Aramaic word for "Lord," which appears in the first part of the verse. The name used in the latter part of the verse is not *Mariah* but *Eshoa*, "Jesus."

Apollos was an Alexandrian Jew. He was a believer in Jesus but not a disciple. He belonged to a sect that still held to the baptism and the teaching of John the Baptist. Although many of John's followers believed in Jesus, they were still identified as John's disciples. And some of them, although friendly toward Jesus' gospel, were not fully under the guidance of the Spirit. These disciples of John had not received the Holy Spirit that comes from being baptized in the name of Jesus. Once they were baptized in Jesus' name, they were ready to be baptized in the spirit.

At present, there are about ten thousand of these people in Iraq. They are called "the people of St. John" and are also known as Sabians. They believe in Jesus but baptize according to John's baptism. They knew nothing about the baptism of the spirit. John's baptism represented repentance for the forgiveness of sin.[14]

In the Near East, a man is baptized many times. To these people, baptism is like taking a bath. They know nothing about the Holy Spirit. When Paul was in Ephesus, he had baptized and laid his hands on some of Apollos' followers and they received the Holy Spirit.[15] Up until this event, these followers lacked power. This is why Paul, at the outset, did not recognize them as followers of Jesus.

---

[13] Acts 18:25, Aramaic Peshitta text, Lamsa translation
[14] See Lk. 3:3-14.
[15] Acts 19:1-6.

CHAPTER 19

PROPHECY

And when Paul laid his hands upon them, the Holy Ghost came on them; and they spake with tongues and prophesied. Acts 19:6.

In Greek, the term "prophecy" means "to tell something in advance," "to foretell." In Aramaic, the word for "prophet" is *newia*, from the root *naba*, "to give out, to gush, spring forth."

These new converts were followers of John the Baptist. They had heard John preach his "baptism of repentance." John had not shown them the way or even promised them any reward. He frankly told people that he was neither the Messiah nor a prophet but a messenger of the one who was coming after him. This one was sent by God and would baptize them with the Holy Spirit and fire. The baptism of Spirit was to remove all sins and make each person a new creation.

When these followers of the Baptist heard Paul, they believed in his message and were baptized in the name of Jesus; that is, they accepted the teaching of Jesus and that he was the promised Messiah, the son of the living God. When Paul laid his hands on them, the Spirit of the Lord God came upon them. They were completely changed. Immediately, they began praising God and confessing Jesus as their Lord and Messiah. Then, they prophesied that there would be a great future and the gospel of the kingdom that Jesus taught was the answer for the ills of the world. They saw that Jesus' method was the only way for peace and harmony—the true meaning of salvation—for the Jewish nation as well as the Gentile nations. They saw a new, spiritual kingdom and their concept of a political kingdom concerning Israel was changed. These converts, through inspiration, had a glimpse of a better world order.

"Laying on of hands" is an ancient Near Eastern custom. Hebrew prophets, while blessing and consecrating kings and other prophets, laid their hands on these candidates so that they would feel the Spirit of God within them. Semites believe that when a holy man lays his hand on them, he becomes a connecting point between them and God. The term "laying on of hands" also means "to accuse, arrest."[1]

DESCENDANTS OF THE TEN TRIBES

And he went into the synagogue, and spake boldly for the space of three months, disputing and persuading the things concerning the kingdom of God. But when divers were hardened and believed not, but spake evil of that way before the multitude, he departed from them, and separated the disciples, disputing daily in the school of one Tyrannus. Acts 19:8-9.

The Aramaic text reads: "Then Paul entered into the synagogue and spoke openly for a period of three months, persuading the people concerning the kingdom of God. But some of them were stubborn and they disputed and cursed the way of God in the presence of the assembly. Then Paul withdrew and separated the disciples from them, and he spoke to them daily in the school of a man named Tyrannus."[2]

Jewish people in this part of Asia Minor were largely descendants of the Ten Tribes and not just Jews from Judea. Some of them already had been baptized in the manner that John the Baptist practiced and therefore were friendly to Paul. These people belonged to the Jewish faith but they did not follow the Mosaic laws too strictly. Nor were they strong supporters of Jewish institutional laws. Like the Galileans, they neglected to observe some of the Jewish traditions.

There were also certain Palestinian Jews from Judea who were bitter against Paul. They disputed his teaching concerning Jesus, whom their Judean co-religionists had condemned and delivered to the Romans. In the beginning, they welcomed Paul and invited him to speak to them and were eager to hear news from Palestine. They were not fully aware of his teaching and mission until they heard him

---

[1] See Acts 6:6, Part 2—"Laying on of Hands," p 57, in this commentary.
[2] Acts 19:8-9, Aramaic Peshitta text, Lamsa translation.

preach about Jesus of Nazareth.

At that time in the Near East, it took a long time for news to travel. Paul's conversion to Jesus' gospel of the kingdom was not known in Asia Minor. The Jews who were living among the Gentiles were not well informed of what was going on in Jerusalem.

PATCHES USED FOR HEALING

So that from his body were brought unto the sick handkerchiefs or aprons, and the diseases departed from them, and the evil spirits went out of them. Acts 19:12.

The Aramaic text reads: "And God wrought great miracles by the hands of Paul, So that even when from the clothes on his body, pieces of garments were brought and laid on the sick, diseases were cured and even the insane were restored."[3]

In this verse, the Aramaic word *ruqaea* refers to pieces of old garments (patches) that were used for mending clothes. Men never wore aprons, nor could they afford to give such garments away. In countries where fabric is woven by hand and scarce, people mend their clothes. Even the rich refuse to give their garments away when they are worn out. They mend them with new or old pieces of cloth.

The mending of clothes is so common that no one is embarrassed or disturbed, no matter how many patches of different colors and material one may have on the trousers. Some clothes are so patched that at times it is difficult to tell what the original fabric really was. Also, when a garment is so worn out that it cannot be mended, it is cut up and used for mending other clothing. On one occasion, Jesus illustrated his teaching by referring to the use of new cloth to mend an old garment.[4]

Paul, like the apostles, had the gift of healing. On his journeys, he performed a number of miracles. His fame as a healer had spread

---

[3] Acts 19:11-12, Aramaic Peshitta text, Lamsa translation.
[4] Mt. 9:16; Mk. 2:21, Lk. 5:36.

so widely that people who could not come to him were satisfied just to have a small piece from one of his old garments. Once again, it was their faith in Jesus, and trust in Paul as one sent by the living Christ, that healed them. The cloth did not contain any healing power.

(Similarly, when Peter walked among the crowds of people, some brought their sick and laid them on the ground so that his shadow might fall on them.[5] Again, it was people's faith that healed the sick and not Peter's shadow.)

Garments of certain noted bishops and religious men who practice healing are considered sacred. Pieces of garments and portions of the Scripture written on parchment or paper are carried great distances for healing purposes. People have such strong faith in the healer that they believe that even a piece of cloth from his garment or a prayer written on paper by him will heal the sick and restore the mentally ill. They understand that the piece of garment is merely a material object. What helps them is their faith in the healer and the thoughts concerning his power that are aroused by the cloth. This token helps to establish the contact that strengthens the faith of the sick in the healer and his power.

Some healers living in far-off and isolated places bless water so that the sick person may wash the afflicted parts of his body with it. The sacred water is mixed with other water and used for bathing the sick. This also serves to strengthen their faith.

Shrines and even graves of certain holy men are constantly visited for healing purposes. Near Easterners believe that the power to heal does not die with the healer but remains forever.

Undoubtedly, this practice of visiting the healer became established because of the difficulty of traveling. In the East, holy men are always prey to the attacks of bandits and members of rival religions and therefore cannot travel to see all the sick in person. So the sick must travel to see the healers. Believers who were ill could persevere through the difficulties and hardships of travel by their deep-seated faith. This kind of faith contributed much toward their

---

[5] Acts 5:15.

cure.

Certain healers just speak a word of comfort and assure the sick of quick results. Some afflicted men travel more than a thousand miles to reach a healer or a special shrine. Since traveling was not customary, the journey was probably the first in their lives. The change, as well as the faith required to make the trip, quickens the restorative healing powers that exist in every individual.

Paul was sought by many men and women who needed his help spiritually, mentally and physically. He could not be present everywhere at once. At times, he could not travel at all because of the lack of funds and the danger to his life. This is the reason he allowed people to have a piece of his tattered garments. He felt compelled to do something, if only in a small way. Paul wanted to help those who were seeking him out to relieve their suffering.

TALISMAN

Then certain of the vagabond Jews, exorcists, took upon them to call over them which had evil spirits the name of the Lord Jesus saying, We adjure you by Jesus whom Paul preacheth. Acts 19: 13.

The Aramaic text reads: "Now certain Jews who went about exorcising evil spirits invoked the name of our Lord Jesus over those who were possessed, saying, We adjure you in the name of Jesus whom Paul preaches."[6]

In many areas of the Near East, diseases are attributed to evil spirits, especially by those practicing magic and sorcery. They claim that evil spirits have babies and that, after dusk, they purposely leave their babies on the streets so that men may step on them and injure them. Some people believe that those who carry charms written by a healer are immune from attacks by these evil forces and that evil spirits injured by men avenge themselves on others who possess no means of protection. Many mothers, out of fear, rush to healers to

---

[6]Acts 19:13, Aramaic Peshitta text, Lamsa translation.

obtain charms written on parchment, which they sew into the garments of their children to protect them from illness.

When a sick person is brought before an exorcist or medium, the latter opens a book and tells the patient that he has injured a certain baby belonging to a clan of evil spirits. Then the exorcist prescribes a remedy, such as sacrificing a sheep to appease the spirits, distributing some of the meat to the poor, and giving the hide and a part of the meat to him. The one who is sick will also have to repeat certain complicated formulas and take oaths many times, mentioning the names of certain spirits, and pledge that he will never again cause injury to their babies. The doctrine of jinn (evil spirits) is prevalent among certain Muslims, especially in Arabia and Persia (Iran).

These are some of the ancient, deep-rooted, superstitious beliefs still held by many simple and credulous men and women. So it was with a few Jews at this time who were practicing sorcery and magic. They were impressed with Paul's power and observed how he worked with the people. So these exorcists imitated his style of healing.

FALSE HEALERS

And the evil spirit answered and said, Jesus I know, and Paul I know; but who are ye? Acts 19:15.

"And there were seven sons of one Sceva, a Jew, and chief of the priests, who did this. And the insane man answered, saying to them, Jesus I recognize and Paul I know: but who are you?[7]

In the Near East, ministers and other religious men are commonly recognized as healers of the mentally and emotionally ill. Their authority and reputation in this field are well established. In many cases, the services of some distinguished healer in one locality are sought by people from other places. His fame spreads so rapidly and widely that the sick and those afflicted with emotional problems

---

[7]Acts 19:14-15, Aramaic Peshitta text, Lamsa translation.

are brought from distant regions and countries to seek healing from his hands. Prior to the visit, the insane are told all about the healer and the powers he possesses. Their minds are prepared before they are brought into his presence.

The mentally ill were easily annoyed and were always wary of false healers who posed as men of God, prescribing physical pain to drive out their illness. As this sort of healing was a form of sorcery performed through physical means, including bodily tortures, its effectiveness was doubted by those who were unbalanced and who sought spiritual healing and comfort. Thus, the insane would often scream and become violent when approached by some men who pretended to be healers. In spite of this, when the mentally ill were in the presence of true men of God and genuine healers, they usually remained calm.

The insane man recognized that the sons of the high priest were not true healers but magicians and sorcerers. When approached by them, he became violent and cried out saying: "I know about Jesus and Paul, but who are you?" He knew Paul was a genuine healer and preacher of the gospel of the living Christ. He had heard about Paul and his miracles of healing and he had been eager to receive healing and comfort through his hands. Therefore, the insane man jumped to his feet and tore the garments of these pretenders. It was the mentally ill man who talked and acted out his anger against them and not a spirit or demon as stated in the King James Version.

BURNING BOOKS OF SORCERY

Many of them also which used curious arts brought their books together, and burned them before all men: and they counted the price of them, and found it fifty thousand pieces of silver. Acts 19:19.

Semites revere their sacred literature and consider it as the basis of their religion. The authority and authenticity of Scripture is never questioned. Members of every faith live according to the beliefs, practices and teachings as contained in their sacred writings.

Nevertheless, when members of one faith decide to change their religion and accept another faith, they burn all of their former sacred literature and renounce their old beliefs, traditions and customs.

Some of them destroy their shrines and places of worship and even change their own names to conform with the new faith that they have adopted. (Also, during wars and persecutions, churches and sacred literature are destroyed.) When theological differences between the two sects are of a minor nature, the converts preserve their literature and rewrite the minor points of conflict.

Converts to a new religion destroy their sacred writings and other symbols of their former faith as a sign of loyalty to their new-found faith and its teachings. Near Easterners on such occasions attempt to show their utmost loyalty and sincerity both inwardly and outwardly by forgetting the old practices and theologies and learning the new ones. However, some religious authorities demand these things from their converts. For example, when a Christian becomes a Muslim, he must destroy his wine and any swine he may own, because Muslims cannot drink wine nor eat pork.

IMAGES OF DIANA

So that not this our craft is a danger to be set at nought; but also that the temple of the great goddess Diana should be despised and her magnificence should be destroyed, whom all Asia and the world worshippeth. Acts 19:27.

"So that not only is this craft doomed, but also the temple of the great goddess Artemis will be disregarded, and the goddess of all Asia Minor, even she whom all peoples worship, will be despised."[8]

The worship of Diana (Artemis), like other Babylonian cults that had been adopted by the people of the Eastern Mediterranean, was declining. The goddess, who supposedly had come down from heaven, was gradually losing her influence. Rivalry among the priests

---

[8]Acts 19:27, Aramaic Peshitta text, Lamsa translation.

of some of these cults created doubt in the minds of the people. There were other contributing factors. The number of Jewish settlers in this part of Asia Minor was increasing and new religions and philosophies were introduced.

The Jewish religion exerted no little influence on the lives of these people. Some of the Gentiles, not being content with their own faiths, had openly joined the synagogues, as in the case of Titus.[9] The Gentiles were searching for something deeper and more tangible. Roman law and good government had brought peace and freedom into Asia Minor, and the people were free to join any religion that they decided was best for them.

The religion of Diana had degenerated into a system of sorcery and had become purely commercial. The priests and artisans derived comfortable incomes from countless silver statues that they made. The artisans sold these images to the people who came from all regions of Asia Minor to worship in the shrine of the goddess. The number of silversmiths employed in this art was so large that they had formed a league to protect their business interests. Some of the beautiful idols were exported; others were offered as gifts at the temple of the goddess.[10]

Paul denounced the images of the goddess Diana. He persuaded the people not to believe in them. The craftsmen saw the danger of losing all of their lucrative business. They began a riot and brought Paul and his companions before the city magistrates.

The Ephesians valued their goddess, and the silversmiths their image-making business, more than the truth. Like the people of Gadara, they were afraid that this new spiritual movement would destroy their means of livelihood.[11]

The sale of statues is still common among many religions and even some Christian sects. Millions of images of the Virgin Mary, Jesus, Joseph, the apostles and saints are sold in various parts of the

---

[9]Acts 18:7.
[10]Some of these images were discovered by an Englishman, Sir Woods, about 100 years ago.
[11]See Mt. 8:28-34.

world. Even today, Palestinian craftsmen manufacture and sell many religious objects in Bethlehem and Jerusalem. Tons of beads and other relics, some of which are imported from Czechoslovakia, are blessed and sold to foreign tourists. Muslims are strongly opposed to this ancient practice and, like Paul, despise statue vendors.

THE GODDESS DIANA

But when they knew that he was a Jew, all with one voice about the space of two hours cried out, Great is Diana of the Ephesians. And when the townclerk had appeased the people, he said, Ye men of Ephesus, what man is there that knoweth not how that the city of the Ephesians is a worshipper of the great goddess Diana, and of the image which fell down from Jupiter? Acts 19:34-35.

Diana (Artemis), the great Ephesian goddess, was venerated throughout Asia Minor. In the Aramaic Peshitta text she is spoken of as the "Great Artemis," whose image had fallen from heaven.

In those ancient days, when people were living in ignorance and darkness, legends about gods and goddesses who had come down from heaven were common. Every god and idol had a legend, especially those that were imported from Babylon and Egypt.

In early times, the Hebrews were often deceived by these legends and worshiped images of the gods of other nations. For example, King Solomon, with all his wisdom, was misled by the worship of Ashtoreth, the Syrian goddess.[12] Jeremiah admonished the Jews who had forsaken God and were worshiping and burning incense to the Queen of heaven.[13]

Ashtoreth was the goddess of the Sidonians in Syria. She was worshiped by the Jews in Egypt and Pathros. Syrians were great merchants. Their ships sailed all the known seas. Wherever they went they introduced their culture and religion. Rachael, Jacob's wife,

---

[12] 1 Ki. 11:5.
[13] Jer. 44:17.

stole some of her father's images of Syrian (Aramean) gods and brought them to Palestine.[14]

Assuredly, religion and civilization of the East exerted a steady influence on the life of the people who inhabited regions around the Mediterranean. The worship of Diana was one among many other influences from the Near East that were spreading westward.

All the pagan gods and goddesses were supposed to have either come from heaven or been the representatives of heavenly bodies. An old Muslim legend upheld by the millions of followers of Islam states that the block of stone at the Kabba in the city of Mecca came down from heaven during the time of Abraham. The stone is worshiped by thousands of pilgrims who visit the holy shrine every year. Some of these men claim that the stone hangs between heaven and earth. As no Christians are permitted to visit the city of Mecca, this story cannot be verified. Some people say the stone is a portion of a meteor. However that may be, legends of this kind are still found in many parts of the world.

---

[14]Gen. 31:34.

CHAPTER 20

PAUL AT TROAS

And upon the first day of the week, when the disciples came together to break bread, Paul preached unto them, ready to depart on the morrow; and continued his speech until midnight. And there were many lights in the upper chamber, where they were gathered together. And there sat in a window a certain young man named Eutychus, being fallen into a deep sleep; and as Paul was long preaching, he sunk down with sleep and fell down from the loft, and was taken up dead. And Paul went down, and fell on him, and embracing him said, Trouble not yourselves; for his life is in him. Acts 20:7-10.

Part 1—BREAKING OF BREAD. *Had-beshaba* in Aramaic means "the first day of the week." The last day of the week is called the Sabbath, the seventh day. According to Scripture, this is the day that the Lord God had ordained as the day of rest.[1] Jesus and his disciples and their followers kept the Sabbath. They fasted and went to the temple to pray like other Jews.

Jewish and Gentile Christians broke bread on the first day of the week, Sunday. They could not meet for instructions on the Sabbath because it was the Jewish holy day. Jewish people rested from all their labors on that day. Some of them even refused to walk or to answer a call. Their food was prepared on Friday so that they need not do any manual work on the Sabbath.

Christians met on Sunday not only to worship but also to teach and receive instructions. At this time, a few Scriptures were available, but most of the people were illiterate. The disciples and their followers met for instruction at the homes of certain converts. They brought their food with them, and after the instruction, they broke bread together.

The Semitic term "breaking bread" means "eating or sharing a

---

[1] Ex. 20:10.

meal together." In the Near East, bread is baked in round, thin loaves. People break it into pieces with their hands and dip it into the dish while eating. They could not do this on the Sabbath, as such an act was regarded as labor, and hence, they would be guilty of breaking the Sabbath law.

Part 2—LAMPS. "Now there was a great glow of light from the torches in the upper chamber where we were gathered together."[2] Earthen lamps are still in use in many countries where kerosene and electricity are unknown. Nomad tribesmen in Kurdistan and the Arabian desert light their tents by burning wood or grass. The glow is sufficient only to light the central part of the tent where people sit on divans conversing with each other. Once in a while they have an opportunity to see each other between tiny pillars of smoke.

During public meetings and weddings, candles made of wax or a torch made of cloth covered with fat are burning in the rooms. These lights are placed on the walls. On such occasions, the house must be lighted as brightly as possible. Large tents and houses require several lamps, candles or torches.

Undoubtedly, the house where this meeting was held was very large and well lighted. People could see the speaker very easily. Paul's fame had spread in these regions and consequently many men and women wanted to see and hear him.

Part 3—THE UPPER ROOM. "And a young man named Eutychus was sitting at the window above and listening, and as Paul prolonged his speech, the youth fell into a deep sleep, and while asleep he fell down from the third loft, and was taken up as dead. And Paul went down and bent over him and embraced him and said, Do not be excited for he still lives."[3]

An upper room is generally built over another room, or on one end of the roof of a house. Its roof is level with those of adjoining houses. However, there are some upper rooms built one over another in Western style. In this case it was a loft.

---

[2]Acts 20:8, Aramaic Peshitta text, Lamsa translation.
[3]Acts 20:9-10, Aramaic Peshitta text, Lamsa translation.

The room in which this meeting took place was in a three-story building—that is, two upper rooms (lofts) built over a house adjoining another house or a slope. Young men could climb, lean and look into the room from one of the front windows or from the window on the roof.

Paul was preaching and presenting a very long talk, but it was interesting to the disciples who were eager to learn all they could about Jesus. Paul visited these cities only once in several years, so he had many things to share with them. Semites never tire of listening to long talks. Missionaries and preachers who speak for several hours are admired and considered learned men. Preachers who are brief lose their reputation as a good speaker.

Part 4—EUTYCHUS INJURED NOT DEAD. One-story dwellings are more usual in Mesopotamia, Palestine and Arabia where Western civilization has not penetrated. But in Cilicia and some other regions of Asia Minor, two- or three-story houses, like the type mentioned above in Part 3, are very common.

In the Near East, social and business conversations used to be carried on through the chimney or the window with many meetings held on the roof.[4] When public meetings or some forms of entertainment are transpiring in the house, curious young men watch through the chimney or the front window. They could easily slip or fall and become badly injured.

Eutychus, while dozing, slipped into a deep sleep and lost his balance. Immediately, he fell to the ground and was seriously hurt. Some of the men at this gathering picked him up and thought he was dead. Paul rushed to help him. And after he had embraced him, he told everyone that the young man was alive and not dead. Paul healed the young man from the injuries that he had sustained from the fall. The apostle Paul had the power to raise Euytchus from his unconscious state.

"Dead" in this verse means "unconscious," as in the incident when

---

[4] 1 Sam. 9:26.

Paul was thought to be dead.[5] Semites describe a person who is seriously injured or extremely ill as being dead. Some men, when summoning a healer or a doctor, in order to rush him to the sick person will say: "The patient is dead; do not trouble yourself to come."

Near Eastern doctors and healers are never alarmed or in a hurry. They know that Easterners are frightened when a member of a family is injured or seriously ill. If an individual were actually dead, they would not send for a doctor.

PAUL ADMONISHES JEWS AND ARAMEANS

Testifying both to the Jews, and also to the Greeks, repentance toward God, and faith toward our Lord Jesus Christ. Acts 20:21.

The Aramaic text reads: "Thus testifying both to the Jews and to the Arameans about repentance toward God and faith in our Lord Jesus Christ."[6] The majority of the early disciples of Jesus in Asia Minor were Jews and Arameans (Syrians). Paul always spoke at Jewish synagogues. Many Syrians were members of the Jewish faith; others were married to Jewish women, as in the case of Timotheus, whose father was Aramean and whose mother was Jewish.[7]

Paul admonished them to turn to God (repent). The Aramaic word *tyawotha*, "repentance," is a biblical term and is well understood by the Jewish people. Hebrew prophets called on the people to repent, that is, return to God. John the Baptist used this word in his strong admonitions to the Pharisees and Sadducees: "Repent ye; for the kingdom of heaven is at hand."[8] Jesus also used this term when addressing the people.[9] To repent also means to repudiate evil ways and to turn from pagan worship to the living God, ruler of heaven and

---

[5]See Acts 14:19.
[6]Acts 20:21, Aramaic Peshitta text, Lamsa translation.
[7]Acts 16:1.
[8]Mt. 3:2, K. J. V.
[9]Jn. 12:40, Aramaic Peshitta text, Lamsa translation.

earth.

Many of the Jews in this region were bitter against Paul and persecuted him at times, causing him considerable suffering. Paul bids them to turn to God and accept Jesus' gospel of God's everlasting kingdom. Jesus fulfilled the role of the Messiah who was to awaken the Jews and Gentiles to God's ever present kingdom.

WARNED BY THE SPIRIT

And now behold, I go bound in the spirit unto Jerusalem, not knowing the things that shall befall me there; Save that the Holy Ghost witnesseth in every city, saying that bonds and afflictions abide me. Acts 20:22-23.

In times of persecution and danger, Semites consult religious men, seers, and wise men before beginning a journey. On these occasions they pray, meditate and seek God's counsel and guidance. Their prayers are often answered through visions and predictions by men or women who have prophetic gifts.

Jewish kings, before going to war against their enemies or when their land was being invaded, usually consulted with men of God. Saul inquired of the prophet Samuel and was told that he would lose the battle and be slain.[10] The Hebrew kings also inquired of the Lord by means of dreams and by the Urim and Thummim, holy relics possessed by the high priests.[11]

Paul, throughout his last missionary journey, had seen the handwriting on the wall. He had been warned by the Holy Spirit as well as by many disciples of Jesus not to go to Jerusalem. The Jewish religious authorities throughout Asia Minor and Macedonia were seeking his life and were spying on him.[12] Regardless of these warnings, Paul was determined to be present in Jerusalem on the day of Pentecost (see verse 16 of this chapter).

---

[10] 1 Sam. 28:15-20.
[11] 1 Sam. 28:6.
[12] Gal. 2:3-4.

Paul was bound in the spirit—that is, felt a strong, deep conviction to follow his guidance regardless of the cost. He knew that it was dangerous to go to the holy city on a feast day. Hundreds of Jewish leaders from Asia Minor would also be present during Pentecost. In the Near East, holy places are not safe places to visit on feast days. Many people do not come to the feast to worship but for other reasons. Some bring merchandise to sell; others come to buy things they need; still others come to seek their enemies. Men are often murdered during these religious holidays.

(When Palestine was under the Turks, Turkish soldiers patrolled the streets of Jerusalem and kept strict vigilance over holy places. Riots often broke out between the Orthodox and Roman Catholic Christians.)

Jesus was also warned not to go to Jerusalem to attend the feast of tabernacles. But after his brothers (relatives) and followers had gone, he went secretly: "Then the Jews sought him at the feast, and said, Where is he?"[13] Jesus was arrested during Passover.

Paul, like Jesus, set his face toward Jerusalem, entrusting his life in the hands of God. He was carrying with him the gifts that the Christians in Macedonia and Asia Minor had collected for the relief of the saints in Jerusalem.[14] Again, just like Jesus, Paul predicted his own arrest and imprisonment. He told some of his followers that they would never see his face from that time onward.

THE BLOOD OF JESUS

Take heed therefore unto yourselves, and to all the flock, over the which the Holy Ghost hath made you overseers, to feed the church of God which he hath purchased with his own blood. Acts 20:28.

"Take heed therefore to yourselves and to all the flock over which the Holy Spirit has appointed you overseers, to feed the church of

---

[13] Jn 7:10-11.
[14] Rom 15:25-26.

Christ which he has purchased with his blood."[15] The Aramaic text more correctly reads "the church of Christ" and not "the church of God."

A later Monophysite Aramaic text known as the "Peshitto" agrees with both the Greek and King James version, using the term "God" instead of "Christ." This text was slightly revised by Rabulah, bishop of Edessa, and other Monophysite bishops who sought union with the Byzantine church in the fifth and sixth centuries CE.

In the early days of the new spiritual movement, Jesus was not called God. Generally, the two terms that his disciples and followers used were *Maran*, "our lord," and *Eshoa*, "Jesus." Peter, on the day of Pentecost, called his master "Jesus of Nazareth, a man approved of God among you by miracles and wonders and signs."[16]

Jewish disciples of Jesus could not have used the term "God," because in their eyes God was spirit and spirit has no flesh or blood. So God could not "purchase the church with his own blood." It was Jesus of Nazareth who gave his life—that is, shed his blood on the cross—and not God. The term "God" was adopted later when the question of Jesus' divinity and humanity had become an issue of discussion and debate. The Christian church became divided on the issue of Jesus' divinity.

The Church is often referred to as "the bride of Christ." In the Near East, men pay large dowries for their beloved brides. Jesus paid with his own blood. In the book of Revelation, the Church is called the wife of the Lamb (Christ).[17]

Jesus died on the cross as a man. His divinity neither suffered nor died. His divinity—that is, the Christ in him—was not subject to natural laws. Christ existed from the very beginning. The Christ was neither born, nor did the Christ die, but lives forever. This belief is still held by most Christians in the Near East.

---

[15] Acts 20:28, Aramaic Peshitta text, Lamsa translation.
[16] Acts 2:22, K. J. V.
[17] Rev. 19:7; 21:9.

NO SALARIES

I have coveted no man's silver, or gold, or apparel. Acts 20:33.

Ministers and missionaries of the churches in the Near East receive no fixed salaries for their work. Most of them labor in the fields and tend sheep. However, some of them are supported by the contributions of their people. Others regularly receive a portion of the gifts that are offered to the church, consisting of butter, bread, cheese, lambs, milk and cloth.

Some ministers and missionaries receive small gifts of money from pious men and women. Generally, when a priest, bishop, or other high church dignitary is entertained, the host presents him with a small sum of money consisting of silver or gold coins, or a new garment. These gifts, no matter how small they may be, are accepted with gratitude and the giver and his family are blessed. Some bishops and priests refuse to accept money, especially if they believe the gift is offered for ulterior motives. When Simon offered the apostle Peter a gift of money, the latter declined it and rebuked the giver for his wrong intentions.

Paul earned his livelihood by the work of his own hands. He was a saddlemaker.[18] On some occasions, nevertheless, Paul did receive money from Christians in Macedonia, especially when he was in prison in Rome. But on the whole, Paul did not burden the congregations that he had organized.

Paul was independent and above reproach in money matters. There were many false teachers and so called "evangelists" who preyed on the faithful and against whom Paul issued warnings.[19] However, the apostles and the gospel workers were entitled to receive generous support from the congregations to whom they ministered. Jesus said that a worker is worthy of his daily bread.

---

[18]See Acts 18:3, Aramaic Peshitta text, Lamsa tranlation.
[19]1 Tim. 3:3; Titus 1:10-11.

LOST DOCUMENTS

I have shewed you all things, how that so labouring ye ought to support the weak, and to remember the words of the Lord Jesus, how he said, It is more blessed to give than to receive. Acts 20:35.

"I have showed you all things, how that one must work hard and be mindful of the weak and remember the words of our Lord Jesus, how he said, It is more blessed to give than to receive."[20] This saying of Jesus is not found in the four canonical gospels—Matthew, Mark, Luke and John.

It is very likely that Paul quoted from other writers. Some of these documents were destroyed during the persecutions that began under the reign of Nero in 64 CE and lasted until the time of Constantine I in 318 CE. We must not overlook the fact that many documents containing the teachings of Jesus were rejected when the New Testament canon was set many years after Paul's death. Others were destroyed by rival church factions and a great many scrolls were excluded for certain reasons.

During the apostolic period, writing in Aramaic was common. The apostles sent pastoral letters to Christians in Antioch and Asia Minor. "And they wrote letters by them after this manner...."[21] "As for the believers among the Gentiles, we have written that they should abstain from the things sacrificed to idols and from fornication, and from what is strangled, and from blood."[22]

These letters and many other documents written by the apostles are now lost. Even Paul had other epistles and writings, some of which perished during the persecutions; other were simply lost. Considering the difficulties of those times, it is a miracle that any of the sacred literature survived and was handed down from one generation to another.

This verse points out that both the giver and the receiver are

---

[20] Acts 20:35, Aramaic Peshitta text, Lamsa translation.
[21] Acts 15:23.
[22] Acts 21:25, Aramaic Peshitta text, Lamsa translation.

blessed. The former is blessed spiritually and the latter receives material blessing. His prayers are answered and his needs met.

CHAPTER 21

PHOENICIA

And finding a ship sailing over unto Phoenicia, we went aboard, and set forth. Acts 21:2.

Phoenicia is the Greek name for *Sur*, "Tyre," an important port in Syria not very far from Galilee. This city was famous for its dyes, especially purple. The Phoenicians were noted for the manufacture of the best cloth, steel, brass and other goods.

The name of the city is derived from the occupation of its people. Syrians were famous for building ships, temples and palaces. They were also noted for the hard steel that they made. Damascus swords were sought by European monarchs when the steel industry was unknown in Europe.

TYRE

And when we had finished our course from Tyre, we came to Ptolemais, and saluted the brethren, and abode with them one day. Acts 21:7.

Tyre was one of the most important Syrian seaports on the Mediterranean Sea. The city was close to Palestine. In ancient times, Tyre, then called Sur, was the capital of Syria. During the reign of King Hiram, the little kingdom cooperated with King Solomon in his great enterprise, when he undertook to build the temple at Jerusalem.[1] For many centuries, this city was a dyeing center.

Jesus had preached in the vicinity of Tyre and Sidon. And these cities were visited by Christian missionaries from Damascus and Jerusalem. The people of this region spoke Aramaic. Undoubtedly,

---

[1] 1 Ki. 5:4-5.

there were a great many Christian converts in Syria. The country was a connecting link between the East and the West. The caravans from Egypt and Mesopotamia passed through it, and Christians from various parts of Asia Minor and Egypt met there. Paul, being a native of Cilicia, in Northern Syria, was at home in this region.

VIRGINS

And the same man had four daughters, virgins, which did prophesy. Acts 21:9.

The Aramaic word *b'thulatha*, "virgins," in this verse means "maidens," that is, "unmarried women." It is rather unusual for a man to have four daughters who had vowed to remain single. In families where the number of children is large, one of the girls may take a vow and remain single for the remainder of her life. In some cases the pledge is made with the father's consent.[2]

The four maidens might have been too young to be married. On the other hand, Philip was an evangelist; the daughters may have been engaged in teaching and preaching and evidently had the gift of prophecy. They taught and warned people of forthcoming events.

PREPARING FOR A JOURNEY

And after those days we took up our carriages, and went up to Jerusalem. Acts 21:15.

"After those days we made our preparations and went up to Jerusalem."[3] In this verse, "carriages" refers to luggage and not vehicles. The Greek word used here is *aposkeuasament*, "having packed the baggage."

---

[2] Compare 1 Cor. 7:36-38.
[3] Acts 21:15, Aramaic Peshitta text, Lamsa translation.

Travelers in the Near East could not travel at their will; they had to wait until a caravan was going to the city that they wanted to visit. It was dangerous to travel alone or even with a few companions. Also, before beginning a journey, travelers hired animals for transport, changed their money and baked bread.

Paul and his companions had only a few pieces of baggage with them that consisted of sacred scrolls and bread. They were following the teaching of Jesus recorded in the gospel of Matthew. Jesus had told his disciples not to carry luggage.[4] At that time, Near Easterners did not take suitcases, extra pairs of shoes, shaving kits and other things that Western people bring with them on a journey.

Travelers in the Near East used to carry from thirty to fifty specially baked loaves of bread, several pounds of cheese, baked and dried fish and other articles of food. These were necessary and had to be obtained before beginning a trip. Sometimes it took several days to make preparations.

Paul was also carrying the money that had been donated by Christians in Asia Minor and Macedonia for fellow Christians in Judea. He had to be very cautious because he could be attacked by bandits. Jerusalem was a six to seven days' journey from Tyre.

TERMINATING A VOW

Do therefore this that we say to thee: We have four men which have a vow on them; Them take, and purify thyself with them, and be at charges with them, that they may shave their heads: and all may know that those things, whereof they were informed concerning thee, are nothing: but that thou thyself also walkest orderly, and keepest the law. Acts 21:23-24.

"Do, therefore, what we tell you. We have four men who have vowed to purify themselves; Take them and go purify yourself with them, and pay their expenses so that they may shave their heads; then everyone will know that what has been said against you is false. And

---

[4]Mt. 10:9-10.

that you yourself have fulfilled the law and obey it."[5]

People often make vows when they are far away from their homes and sacred shrines. Sometimes they make vows to abstain from certain things until they worship at a certain shrine. They may also fast and make a vow when they pray for the recovery of a sick person, the birth of a child, a victory over enemies or when returning from a long journey.

"And Jephthah vowed a vow unto the Lord, and said, If thou shalt without fail deliver the children of Ammon into my hands, that it shall be, that whatsoever cometh forth of the doors of my house to meet me, when I return in peace from the children of Ammon, shall surely be the Lord's, and I will offer it up for a burnt offering."[6]

People may also vow with a curse so that no one would dare to break it. Saul put a curse on anyone who ate food before evening.[7] His son Jonathan broke the vow, but he was forgiven.[8]

All Hebrew Nazarites made vows. They had to abstain from strong drink and from cutting their hair.[9] Letting their hair grow was a constant reminder of the vow. They were distinguished from other people by their long hair.

Samson believed in the vow and trusted that his strength was in letting his hair grow. When Samson lost his hair, he also lost his strength because when his hair was cut, he knew that the sacred vow had been broken.[10]

These four men had vowed not to shave their heads (cut their hair) until a certain time. They may have just arrived from far-off countries to worship in the temple at Jerusalem. Paul was instructed by the apostles to pay the expenses of their purification and hair cutting. This was done to show that Paul was not against the Mosaic

---

[5] Acts 21:23-24, Aramaic Peshitta text, Lamsa translation.
[6] Judges 11:30-31, K. J. V.
[7] 1 Sam. 14:24.
[8] 1 Sam. 14:45.
[9] Num. 6:3-5; Judges 13:7-14.
[10] Judges 16:19.

law or the Jewish customs.¹¹

Reports had been circulated that Paul had been preaching to the Jews in Asia Minor in opposition to the law of Moses and other Jewish religious customs.¹² The apostles wanted to avoid any serious break between the Christian Jews and Paul. This was also a warning to Paul to be careful in his attacks on Jewish theology, for Paul personally had no use for some of the Jewish traditions and ordinances.¹³

PAUL IN THE TEMPLE

Then Paul took the men, and the next day purifying himself with them, entered into the temple, to signify the accomplishment of the days of purification, until that an offering should be offered for every one of them. Acts 21:26.

Most of the Jewish feasts lasted a week. Jewish rituals were long and the ceremonials and ordinances were many. Visitors had to change their money for temple money,¹⁴ buy sacrifices, purify themselves before presenting their offerings, and perform various other duties according to the law. Those who had made vows were required to have their hair cut and then the hair was burned in the fire under the sacrifice. A priest took a portion of the sacrifice and other gifts, placed them in the hands of the person who had vowed, and then offered it to the Lord.¹⁵ Such were the laws of the Nazarites and their vows.

Paul also had made a vow which was fulfilled when he was at Cenchrea.¹⁶ Now he was sent by the apostle James to accompany four converts who had made vows. He was told to do this to silence the

---

¹¹Num. 6:13-14.
¹²Acts 21:21.
¹³Col. 2:16-17.
¹⁴"Temple money" means "temple coins." These coins had no graven images.
¹⁵Num. 6:18-19.
¹⁶Acts 18:18.

rumors that were being circulated against him by Jewish Christians.[17] But his visit to the temple and his subsequent participation in the ceremonies led to his arrest and imprisonment.

PAUL MISTAKEN

And as Paul was to be led into the castle, he said unto the chief captain, May I speak unto thee? Who said, Canst thou speak Greek? Acts 21:37.

After the revolt under Ishmael, about 585 BCE, a large number of Jews fled to Egypt because they feared the Chaldeans. These Jews remained in Egypt during the period of the Babylonian and Persian empires.

After the fall of the Persian empire, in the latter part of the fourth century BCE, the Greeks conquered Egypt. They built new cities and tried to develop the country. As a result, the Jews in Egypt increased and prospered during this time. Being a small minority, they clung together and succeeded in preserving their religion and racial customs, but they lost their language.

The Hebrew tongue in Alexandria and other large commercial centers was replaced with Greek. It was during the Greek rule over Egypt that the Septuagint was made. This was a translation of the Hebrew Bible into Greek. But the work was condemned by the Palestinian Jews; they declared a day of mourning as a protest against the new version, branding it unreliable and inaccurate.

The Roman captain mistook Paul for an Egyptian Jew. This is the reason he asked Paul if he could speak Greek. "Art not thou that Egyptian, which before these days madest an uproar, and leddest out into the wilderness four thousand men that were murderers?"[18]

The Jews in Palestine and Syria did not speak Greek. In his book *The Wars of the Jews,* Josephus informs us that Greek was not spoken

---

[17] Acts 21:20-21.
[18] Acts 21:38, K. J. V.

in Palestine and that only a few men who tried to learn it were rewarded for their efforts. Jews in Judea spoke a Chaldean dialect or southern Aramaic, and the Galileans spoke northern Aramaic. Paul, being a learned man, could speak both dialects.

HEBREW TONGUE

And when he had given him licence, Paul stood on the stairs, and beckoned with the hand unto the people. And when there was made a great silence, he spake unto them in the Hebrew tongue. Acts 21:40.

"Hebrew" in this verse means "Aramaic"—that is, the Aramaic language spoken by the Jews who are known as members of the Hebrew race. Aramaic replaced Hebrew during the Babylonian captivity in the sixth century BCE. The Jews remained in Babylon about seventy years and gradually lost their native tongue. This linguistic change was inevitable because Hebrew and Aramaic were so closely related. Aramaic was the language that Abraham, Isaac, Jacob and his children spoke before the Hebrew language came into existence. Aramaic was spoken in Palestine prior to the fourth century BCE. The early Hebrews were called Arameans.[19]

After the return from Babylon, the Jews spoke Aramaic. For more than one thousand years, Aramaic remained the language of the Jewish people. Aramaic in Palestine was replaced by another Semitic tongue, Arabic, in the ninth century CE.

When Paul was on his way to Damascus, Jesus, in a vision, spoke to him in Aramaic. This was Paul's mother tongue. Many portions of holy Scripture were written in Aramaic. Jewish prayers and theologies were also written and circulated in Aramaic. Today many prayers in Aramaic are found in Jewish prayer books.

Paul was a scholar. He had studied at Jerusalem under the great teacher and noted scholar Gamaliel and had become a member of the Jewish Sanhedrin. When he addressed the people in his own defense,

---

[19] See Dt. 26:5, Aramaic Peshitta text, Lamsa translation.

he did so in their tongue. His address dealt with his conversion, Jewish history and theological matters that could be best expressed in his own native language.

No doubt, Paul knew some Greek. Some Jews spoke several languages. They needed to know them for business and traveling purposes, but they would not be familiar with theological and legalistic terms in those languages. Roman officials always spoke in the native tongues. English and French officials in Palestine and Syria used to converse in the language of the people over whom they once ruled.

Paul, being in the presence of Roman authorities, might have been expected to speak in Greek, but he did not speak it well enough to explain his case, so he spoke in his own tongue.

CHAPTER 22

RACE AND RELIGION

I am verily a man which am a Jew, born in Tarsus, a city in Cilicia, yet brought up in this city at the feet of Gamaliel, and taught according to the perfect manner of the law of the fathers, and was zealous toward God, as ye all are this day. Acts 22:3.

Part 1—PAUL, A JEW BY FAITH. "I am a Jew" does not mean that Paul was of the tribe of Judah, but rather that he was a member of the Jewish faith. He was a Hebrew of the tribe of Benjamin and was a member of the sect called *Parisheh*, "Pharisees." The Pharisees were nationalists. They believed in the messianic promises and the ultimate restoration of Israel.

Interestingly, when Semites greet each other during business engagements or social events, the first thing they ask is: "What is your *Din* (religion)?" The reason for this is that business and communal activities are conducted according to the protocol that one faith accords to members of another faith. For example, a Muslim cannot lend money with an interest charge to a member of his own faith, but he may lend to a Christian and charge interest if he desires to do so. Also, a treaty or contract between a Muslim and a non-Muslim is not binding.

Another difference in greeting is that a Muslim would be insulted if a person of another faith greeted him in the same manner that another Muslim would salute him. Only a Muslim is permitted to say to another of his faith, *Al salam alekom*, "Peace be with you." Non-Muslims cannot use these words because a Muslim does not consider himself "at peace" with them until they accept Islam.

Paul's race and religion were often in question. At times he declared that he belonged to the sect of the Pharisees. When among Gentiles, he acted and lived as one of them so that he might win them to the teachings of Jesus. The Jews would not have allowed him to speak in their synagogues had they known he was not a strict, observing Jew. His race would not have mattered much because there were many Arameans who had intermarried with the Jews and whose children had adopted the Jewish faith.

Paul showed good judgment. He would wait to disclose his religious connections until the conclusion of his messages and testimonies. He always began with the Jewish fathers and history, climaxing with Jesus as the Messiah/Christ. At the end of Paul's preaching, the Jews might then go into an uproar. But Paul had delivered his message and gained many new supporters for the movement during his talk. On several occasions, however, when he finished speaking, he was beaten and imprisoned.

In the minds of Near Easterners, race and religions are inseparable. No one can be loyal to a race if he tries to weaken its faith and traditions. The race is always governed by the justice and morality derived from its religion. Therefore, disloyalty to the religious dictates would be considered disloyalty to the race and the state.

Part 2—UNDER A TEACHER'S CARE. "At the feet of Gamaliel" means "under his care." In the Near East, when a father entrusts his son to a teacher, he says: "Let him be the servant of your feet." When a teacher enters a house, servants rush to remove his shoes. But during school hours, students may take care of their teachers' shoes, go on errands and perform other menial tasks for them.

Teaching was one of the most respected professions and teachers were highly honored. But desks and chairs were unknown. Up until the 1900s, a teacher sat on a cushion that lay on the ground. He would hold a long stick in his hand, and his pupils would sit around him in a circle. When he stretched out his feet, he could almost touch some of the students.

(Both teachers and students had to remove their shoes during the studies because most of the courses were religious—that is, scriptures were read and prayers were recited.)

Usually, a favorite student would sit directly in front of the teacher. Apparently, Paul was favored by Gamaliel; therefore, as a young man, he sat directly in front of his teacher—that is, directly in front of his feet.

PAUL WARNED

And it came to pass, that when I was come again to Jerusalem, even while I prayed in the temple, I was in a trance; And saw him saying unto me, Make haste, and get thee quickly out of Jerusalem: for they will not receive thy testimony concerning me. Acts 22:17-18.

The phrase "I was in a trance" does not appear in Aramaic, Peshitta manuscripts. It is likely that the translators added it. The Aramaic text reads: "And while praying in the temple, I saw a vision, saying to me. . . . "

What the author of the book of Acts means is that Paul, while praying, was warned by a vision, perhaps similar to the one that Peter saw when he prayed on the roof at Joppa.[1] On other occasions, Paul had similar experiences. He often was guided and directed through visions.[2]

A ROBE

And as they cried out, and cast off their clothes, and threw dust into the air. Acts 22:23.

Generally, when Near Easterners were not working, they wore expensive and heavy robes as a sign of dignity and not out of necessity. The outer robe or garment usually worn on such occasions was called *abaya*.

When men entered a house they removed their *abayas*. Also, while attending a mosque or church gathering, the robe and shoes were removed and set aside. In addition, when quarreling they would take off their robes so they might avoid getting them soiled. A man

---

[1] Acts 10:10.
[2] Acts 23:11.

would rather not risk having a good robe destroyed if he were stabbed in a fight.

The men who were listening to Paul became enraged and, as a signal of protest, they cast off their robes. This also meant that they were ready to attack him and stone him to death as they did Stephen. They made even further protest by throwing dust into the air.

Dust is a symbol of mourning and also a sign of repudiation when a wrong act of some sort is committed. When a man is killed, his relatives throw dust over their heads and garments. Often when some heinous deed is done, Semites will lose their tempers and behave insanely.

Paul, in the eyes of some of the Jews, had defiled the temple by bringing Gentiles into it. The priests and religious men tried to magnify the seriousness of the incident so that they might incite the crowd. These religious authorities wanted Paul arrested, so they demonstrated their protest and anger.

PAUL SCOURGED

The chief captain commanded him to be brought into the castle, and bade that he should be examined by scourging; that he might know wherefore they cried so against him. Acts 22:24.

Usually officials scourged prisoners before a trial. They were beaten at the scene of the crime or on the way to prison. This punishment was administered for two reasons: (1) to quiet the mob and (2) to frighten the prisoner and obtain a quick confession from him.

Pilate, hoping to appease the accusers who brought Jesus to him, ordered Jesus to be scourged in the midst of the trial.[3] Even today, men who are charged with insurrection or other serious crimes are severely punished before they are brought to trial.

Paul was charged with sedition and with being a ringleader of

---

[3]Jn. 19:1-2.

the sect of the Nazarenes. He was also accused of having profaned the temple because he brought uncircumcised Gentiles into it. Both charges were extremely serious.

The first offense was against the Roman government. The second charge was against the Jewish religious laws that were also respected by the Romans. Not even Roman authorities could enter the sacred ground of the inner court of the temple. That area was reserved for the Jews only.

CHAPTER 23

WHITED WALL

Then said Paul unto him, God shall smite thee, thou whited wall; for sittest thou to judge me after the law, and commandest me to be smitten contrary to the law? Acts 23:3.

"Whited wall" is an Aramaic idiom and it means a "hypocrite." It is still used by Semites as an insult when they argue with one another.

Astha is the lower part of the wall, just a little above the foundation. Generally, Near Eastern houses are not painted either on the inside or outside. Nevertheless, because of black soot caused by smoke, the lower part of the wall is often whitened or plastered with white clay to protect the clothing of men or women who may lean against it. The wall looks clean only for a short time. Then it has to be whited again and the black soot covered.

The high priest, whom Paul evidently mistook for an elder, was black within. To Paul, the man who stood before him appeared as a wall that had been painted white but was hiding the black soot underneath. This priest was sitting in judgment to convict others for breaking the laws, when he also was guilty of breaking the law.

"Whited wall" is a casual but scornful rebuke on the part of Paul, who, after being smacked in the face, was unable to control his anger. Jewish law prohibited cursing a priest, so he expressed his anger by calling the high priest a hypocrite. (Jesus also had been slapped on his face when he answered the high priest informally and indifferently, when he said: "Why askest thou me?")

PRIESTS OFTEN MISTAKEN FOR LAYMEN

Then said Paul, I wist not, brethren, that he was the high priest: for it is written, Thou shall not speak evil of the ruler of thy people. Acts 23:5.

In the Near East, Semites do not wear clerical collars or ecclesiastical garments or possess diplomas when they become rabbis or ministers of religion. Priests, mullahs and rabbis dress simply and live like ordinary people except when performing their religious duties; then they dress in ecclesiastical robes and are covered with white mantles. (Some Muslim religious men are an exception to this.) This makes it difficult to distinguish a rabbi or minister from other men. Usually, learned Muslim men wear green turbans.

These men of the cloth normally make a livelihood by working as farmers, merchants, teachers and artisans. Some of them are supported by tithes and gifts given by worshipers. But as the homes of these religious men are often open to the poor and strangers, they are usually impoverished and in want.

Tithes and gifts are not sufficient to maintain religious men who are married. Therefore, most priests and ministers of religion live simply. However, in large cities one may occasionally meet a few of the clergy wearing heavy turbans or some distinguishing garment. But such garments may also be worn by other dignitaries, noblemen and the rich.

Paul did not recognize the high priest as such because his garments were like those of other people. Paul thought that he must be an elder sitting in judgment. Often, elders, priests or any dignitary who may be available would settle quarrels and disputes. This was the Near Eastern custom.

Paul called the high priest a hypocrite, but when he saw his mistake, he apologized, saying that he did not realize who he was. The Mosaic law prohibits cursing priests because in those ancient days priests were dedicated to God's work and, therefore, could not be reproached.[1] But in Paul's day, the office of a priest could easily be bought by the highest bidder. Nevertheless, Paul showed his respect and devotion to Jewish law and the high priest. Obeying the laws of the land and respecting those in authority were a part of the early movement of Christianity.

---

[1]Ex. 22:28.

ROMAN OFFICIALS

And he wrote a letter after this manner: Claudius Lysias unto the most excellent governor Felix sendeth greeting. Acts 23:25-26.

During apostolic times, Rome divided Palestine into several small kingdoms that were ruled by native princes appointed by Roman military or provincial authorities and later confirmed by Caesar. The power of these kings was limited in many respects, especially in regard to crimes and political affairs. The native kings had power to collect taxes, maintain law and order and perform other duties in civil matters, but political crimes involving capital punishment were tried by the Romans.

High Roman officials called pro-consuls were stationed in Antioch and other strategic cities in Syria near the Persian border. Roman and Persian armies were strongly fortified and served as spearheads for Roman campaigns in the Euphrates Valley. Therefore, after its occupation by the Romans in 67 BCE, Syria was made a Roman province. High Roman officials resided in Antioch and other important cities that were garrisoned by Roman soldiers. These officials were needed for military operations.

Minor Roman officials, known as procurators (governors), were stationed in Jerusalem and other places to act as advisors to look after native government and to see that taxes were collected. (The Roman rule was similar to the British when they ruled Palestine and Transjordan. Great Britain was represented by high commissioners who resided at Jerusalem and Amman. Other minor civil and military officials with some administrative powers were stationed in smaller places. Native kings and their officials had limited powers, except in religious matters. The countries' foreign policies were determined by the British foreign offices. British citizens were tried in special courts under English law.)

Felix, the Roman governor of Caesarea, had jurisdiction over Palestine and certain parts of Syria. His wife was Jewish and he was well acquainted with Jewish law and customs. Mandatory powers, not having courts in the occupied countries, try their own people at the

Residency (palace).

Paul was a native of Cilicia in Syria. He was a Roman citizen and therefore entitled to Roman protection and justice. The Romans had extraterritorial rights enabling them to be tried in special courts under Roman law. Justice in the native courts was perverted; officials were corrupt and judges easily bought. Had Paul been a citizen of Palestine, the Jewish officials, as in the case of Stephen,[2] could have put him to death by stoning.

Jesus was tried by the Roman governor because he was from Galilee. The Jewish priests and native authorities in Jerusalem had no jurisdiction over Galilee. That region was under Herod.[3] Roman courts were good, but the authorities often sacrificed justice to please native kings and priests.

---

[2]Acts 7:58-59.
[3]Lk. 23:6-7.

CHAPTER 24

NAZARENES

For we have found this man a pestilent fellow, and a mover of sedition among all the Jews throughout the world, and a ringleader of the sect of the Nazarenes. Acts 24:5.

Prior to Paul's conversion and the expansion of the new spiritual movement among the Gentiles—that is, among Arameans, Assyrians, and Arabs—the followers of Jesus were called Nazarenes. (Near Eastern Muslims still called Near Eastern Christians by this name.)[1]

In the Near East, followers of a teacher are called by their teacher's name, and often the teacher is known by the name of his town, especially when there are several other teachers bearing the same name. Many names are connected with a town—for example, Jesus of Nazareth, Joseph of Ramtha, Simon of Cyrene and Mary of Magdala. Even today, many Semites use the names of their towns as surnames.

The term "Christians" was a later term applied to the followers of this new spiritual movement[2] and is a direct translation from Greek. (The term "Christ" means "the anointed one.") The Aramaic word is *M'sheeheh*, meaning "anointed ones," "those who are anointed with oil." The Greek term comes directly from this Aramaic word. As we have said, Arabs today call Christians *nassara,* and the Turks called them *nosrani.* The followers of Islam were nicknamed "Mohammedans," that is, followers of the prophet Mohammed. Today we refer to them as Muslims.

Paul was accused by his enemies of being the ringleader of the Nazarenes, the followers of Jesus of Nazareth. Jesus was also accused as a revolutionary and disturber of the peace in Palestine. He had told

---

[1] Mt. 2:22-23; See Mk. 14:66-67, Aramaic Peshitta text, Lamsa translation.
[2] See Acts 15.

his disciples in advance that they would be persecuted and reviled.[3]

BRIBES WERE COMMON

He hoped also that money should have been given him of Paul, that he might loose him: wherefore he sent for him the oftener, and communed with him. Acts 24:26.

In those days, governorships, judgeships, and other high positions were obtained by paying a large sum of money which was called a present. This custom prevailed in many lands until World War 1. High government officials and judges expected gifts before performing their duties or extending favors. Some people sent gifts a few days before seeking help from the official.[4]

Jesus told his disciples a parable of the poor widow whom the judge refused to see because she had nothing to offer him, but she persisted until she compelled him to do justice for her.[5] The Roman governor, knowing that Paul had a great many followers, expected a large sum of money from him. But Paul had no money with which to bribe him. So Paul stayed in prison until a new governor was appointed.

---

[3] Mt. 5:11, Jn. 15:20
[4] Ex. 23:8, Ps. 26:10.
[5] Lk. 18:2-5.

CHAPTER 26

KING AGRIPPA II

Especially because I know thee to be expert in all customs and questions which are among the Jews: wherefore I beseech thee to hear me patiently. Acts 26: 3.

King Agrippa II was the son of Agrippa I and the great-grandson of Herod the Great. His father, Agrippa I, in order to please the Jewish authorities, had beheaded James, son of Zebedee, and also had attempted to kill Simon Peter.[1]

Agrippa II was educated in Rome and was also well tutored in Jewish law and traditions. Like his father and his great-grandfather, he wanted to win the favor of the Jewish authorities and people. But Herod the Great had been hated by the Jewish populace. He was an Idumean by race but a Jew by faith. His children and grandchildren were brought up according to Jewish law and customs.

Being a Near Easterner and a member of the Jewish faith, King Agrippa II knew that the Jews were divided into several theological schools and that they quarreled over the doctrine of the resurrection of the dead. Paul was a Pharisee and believed in this idea. But the Sadducees did not believe in such teaching and firmly opposed it.

The Pharisees were the largest and strongest party in Palestine, and the Jewish kings nearly always sided with the powerful majorities. The king could have released Paul if he had wanted to do so, but like Pilate he was afraid of losing his position.

Paul appealed to this ruler as one who was well versed in Jewish theologies and Scripture. He showed from holy Scripture that the Messiah/Christ should suffer and that he should be the first to rise from the dead.

King Agrippa II, like other Jewish adherents, believed in the coming of a political Messiah but was not interested in the restoration

---

[1] See Acts 12:1-2.

of the Davidic kingdom. His great-grandfather had exterminated the princes of the Hasmonean dynasty. A Jewish state ruled by a Jewish Messiah was contrary to the policy of the Herodian dynasty.

MESSIAH/CHRIST THE FULFILLMENT

Unto which promise our twelve tribes, instantly serving God day and night, hope to come. For which hope's sake, King Agrippa, I am accused of the Jews. Acts 26:7.

The Aramaic text reads: "It is to the fulfillment of this hope that our twelve tribes expect to arrive by means of earnest prayers day and night. And for this very hope's sake, I am accused by the Jews, O King Agrippa."[2]

The Messiah/Christ was to gather the scattered tribes of Israel who were carried away from their homeland by the Assyrian kings. The Ten Tribes of Israel were to be restored as one nation, but not as before. They were to become one people, a spiritual people set aside by God.

Paul reminded King Agrippa that he was expounding these truths that were promised to Israel's forefathers. This is the reason he was being persecuted by the Jewish leaders. As we have said earlier, King Agrippa was the great-grandson of Herod the Great by his Jewish wife, Princess Marianne. He, like his father and grandfather, was born into and strictly reared in the Judaism of the time. Therefore, Paul addressed him as he would have addressed a Jewish king. Agrippa II was good to the Jewish people.

CHRISTIANS JEWS

And I punished them oft in every synagogue and compelled them to blaspheme; and being exceedingly mad against them, I persecuted them and even unto strange cities. Whereupon as I went to Damascus with authority

---

[2]Acts 26:7, Aramaic Peshitta text, Lamsa translation.

and commission from the chief priests, Acts 26:11-12.

The preaching of Jesus' gospel of God's kingdom was taught first to the Jewish people; therefore, they became the first disciples and followers of the messianic message. They were Palestinian members of the Jewish faith. Jesus had preached and taught in Jewish synagogues and his apostles likewise were permitted to worship and, at times, speak in the synagogues.

At the outset, this new spiritual movement was not regarded as hostile to Judaism. Many Jewish people were sympathetic toward the cause of this movement. Years later, however, the Jewish disciples and followers of Jesus began to establish their own congregations and teach doctrines that were contrary to the traditions of the elders.

Paul was commissioned by the High priest to investigate the Jews who were suspected of being sympathetic toward Christianity and to arrest and punish those found guilty of disloyalty to Judaism. In the early period of the Christian era, the followers of Jesus could hardly be distinguished from the adherents of the Jewish faith.

Christians and Jews wore the same style of clothes and ate only kosher food. Their religious practices, customs and manners were identical. They both worshiped in the temple and attended services in the synagogues. The only difference between those of the Jewish faith and the Jewish Christians was that the followers of Jesus were sympathetic toward the new revelation which, in their eyes, was true Judaism. Jesus had told them that he had not come to destroy the law and the prophets but to fulfill them. Therefore the disciples and followers of the Galilean prophet and Messiah were friendly toward the Jews.

CHAPTER 27

FASTS USED AS A CALENDAR

Now when much time was spent, and when sailing was now dangerous, because the fast was now already past, Paul admonished them. Acts 27:9.

The Aramaic text reads: "There we remained for a long time, till also the day of the Jewish fast was over and, since it had now become dangerous for anyone to sail, Paul gave them advice."[1] In lands where printed calendars were unknown, fast days and festivals are used to reckon time. Priests, deacons and a few elderly men and women keep track of the days and months and inform the people of coming feasts and fast days. Of course, some of the people know when feasts and fasts will fall, for they are the most important events of the year, and people are mindful of them.

Also, feasts and fasts are used as reminders to pay off debts, transact business and travel. Fasting is mentioned here simply to indicate the season of the year that is dangerous for sailing due to bad weather. This Jewish fast falls on the tenth day of the seventh month and is known as the Day of Atonement. On this day people rest from all work and devote their time to fasting and prayer. The fast is followed by the Feast of the Tabernacles observed on the fifteenth day of the seventh month.[2]

PAUL EXHORTS THE PASSENGERS

But after long abstinence Paul stood forth in the midst of them, and said, Sirs, ye should have hearkened unto me, and not have loosed from Crete, and to have gained this harm and loss. And now I exhort you to be of good cheer: for there shall be no loss of any man's life among you, but

---

[1] Acts 27:9, Aramaic Peshitta text, Lamsa translation.
[2] Lev. 23:26-34.

of the ship. Acts 27:21-22.

The Aramaic text reads: "And as no man among them had eaten anything, Paul stood up in the midst of them, and said, Men, if you had listened to me, we would not have sailed from Crete, and we would have been spared this loss and suffering. Now let me counsel you not to be depressed: for not a single life among you will be lost, but only the ship."[3]

Paul was a prisoner on board the ship. In such emergencies, prisoners are not chained, especially those who are imprisoned for minor offenses. Paul was not a criminal. He had appealed to Caesar, and he was on board a ship that was sailing for Rome, where he was to appear before the emperor.

Paul was free to mix with other passengers, and being a preacher of Jesus' gospel of the kingdom and a believer in God, he was encouraging the people during the shipwreck, assuring them that they would be safe. He had warned the captain and the sailors not to leave Crete.[4] Moreover, Paul had been assured by a messenger of God in a dream that he would stand before Caesar and that no one would be lost in the shipwreck.

AN ANGEL COMMUNED WITH PAUL

For there stood by me this night the angel of God, whose I am, and whom I serve, Saying, Fear not, Paul thou must be brought before Caesar: and, lo, God hath given thee all them that sail with thee. Acts 27:23-24.

The Aramaic text reads: "For there has appeared to me this night the angel of God to whom I belong and whom I serve."[5] In his vision, Paul saw a messenger sent from God. The angel gave him counsel and encouragement. The Aramaic word *malakha* means "angel,

---

[3]Acts 27:21-22, Aramaic Peshitta text, Lamsa translation.
[4]Acts 27:10-11.
[5]Acts 27:23, Aramaic Peshitta text, Lamsa translation.

messenger, minister, God's counsel." Through the medium of a dream or vision, God communed with Paul.

Near Eastern people believe that an angel rests upon the right shoulder of an individual to protect, guide and admonish that person. In reality, an angel is God's counsel, which is constantly available to those who trust in God's presence and Spirit. God is the Father of all humanity and continually acts as a father who loves, cares for and protects his children.

CHAPTER 28

BITTEN BY A VIPER

And when Paul had gathered a bundle of sticks, and laid them on the fire, there came a viper out of the heat, and fastened on his hand. Acts 28:3.

Many religious men and women defy the fear of snakes, scorpions and poisonous insects by picking them up in their hands and holding no thought of being harmed by them. These men and women are never disturbed by the sight of such menacing looking and dangerous reptiles and insects.

There are those on whom poison has no harmful effect and therefore are immune from bites. Such persons collect honeycombs from beehives without protecting their faces and hands, and some even handle snakes and scorpions. And, at times, when they are bitten, the poison does not take effect.

These people are always recognized by the public as having some secret power that protects them. People think of them as men of God and healers. Most religious men are not afraid of snakes that are often found in church buildings in the Near East. In some ancient shrines, snakes may even crawl among the worshipers, but they won't attack anyone who does not disturb them. Priests and custodians walk among them and even mistakenly step on them without being harmed.

According to the Aramaic text, Paul was bitten by the viper that hung on his hand. The Aramaic word *nekhtat* derives from the root *nak* and it means "to strike, bite." In Hebrew the word is *nakae*.

When Paul saw the viper hanging from his hand, he was not alarmed. He shook his hand and the viper fell into the fire. The primitive and superstitious islanders immediately thought of him as some sort of a god who was immune from harm. So they began to worship him and bring their sick to him that he might heal them.

Paul, of course, did not know that the viper was among the sticks. He did not deliberately handle the viper just to prove his power. It was accidental; therefore, Paul was divinely protected. The same God who had saved him from the shipwreck saved him from the poisonous viper.

PAUL AS A LEADER

And it came to pass, that the father of Publius lay sick of a fever and a bloody flux: to whom Paul entered in, and prayed, and laid his hands on him, and healed him. So when this was done, others also, which had diseases in the island came, and were healed: Acts 28:8-9.

In places where medicines and doctors are unknown, sick people seek the aid of holy men and the wise. In many regions of the Near East and Asia, American and English missionaries are considered as doctors and are frequently consulted by suffering people. Near Easterners believe that those who can minister to their souls must surely be able to minister to their bodies. On the other hand, illnesses such as fever and dysentery are easily cured.

Paul, though a prisoner, was the wisest man in the entire group and his advice was sought by many who were with him on board the ship. He had predicted the disaster but also had assured the sailors that not one of them would perish. His unusual power was felt by all who talked to him and sought his help. They were greatly impressed when they found that he had the gift of healing. This power seemed especially wonderful to these people, whose faith was almost like little children.

CHRISTIANS IN ROME

Where we found brethren, and were desired to tarry with them seven days: and so we went toward Rome. And from thence, when the brethren heard of us, they came to meet us as far as Appii forum, and The Three Taverns: whom when Paul saw, he thanked God, and took courage. And when we came to Rome, the centurion delivered the prisoners to the captain of the guard: but Paul was suffered to dwell by himself with a soldier that kept him. Acts 28:14-16.

The Aramaic text reads: "Where we found brethren who invited us; and we stayed with them seven days: and then we departed for Rome. When the brethren there heard of us, they came out to meet us as far as the street which is called Appii forum and The Three Taverns. When Paul saw them, he thanked God, and was greatly encouraged. Then we entered Rome, and the centurion gave permission to Paul to live wherever he pleased with a soldier to guard him."[1]

Apparently, some early disciples and followers of Jesus had established a center in Rome. No doubt, most of these people were servants and slaves, Christians and Jews, who had been sold in Roman markets. When Paul landed in southern Italy at Puteoli, he was greeted by these Christian brethren.[2] There was both a Jewish synagogue and a Christian group in the imperial city of Rome.

Paul had been very eager to see these Christians and to lay his hands upon them, thus imparting to them the spiritual gifts such as healing, prophesying, teaching and preaching.

Jesus' fame had traveled to many countries outside of Palestine. Interestingly, groups of Christians were found in many cities in the Roman Empire. The teaching of Jesus and his gospel of God's kingdom was being preached far and wide by merchants, prisoners, soldiers and travelers. Jewish Christians were found everywhere. Some of these men were present in Jerusalem on the day of Pentecost.[3]

Nonetheless, up to this point, the Christian movement had not been well organized in Rome. There were a number of followers and sympathizers among Jews, Syrians (Arameans) and proselytes, but they had no teachers or places of worship of their own. They still attended the synagogue and the Romans thought of them as Jews.

These men had been told about Paul, his work and arrest by the

---

[1] Acts 28:14-16, Aramaic Peshitta text, Lamsa translation.
[2] Acts 28:13.
[3] Acts 2:9-10.

Christians who had come from Greece. Paul met them and the chiefs of the Jews. He discussed with them his imprisonment and persecution. Many of the Jews believed and accepted the new teaching and Jesus as the promised Messiah. But there were others who refused to hear what Paul had to say.

PAUL A HOUSE PRISONER IN ROME

And Paul dwelt two whole years in his own hired house, and received all that came in unto him. Acts 28:30.

The Aramaic text reads: "And Paul hired a house for himself at his own expense and lived in it for two years; there he received all who came to him, Preaching the kingdom of God and teaching openly about our Lord Jesus Christ, without hindrance."[4]

Paul, before his arrival in Rome, met a number of Christians at Puteoli and Appii forum who had come to greet him and assist him. There were a great many Syrian and Jewish Christians in Rome. Some of them were brought from Palestine as captives, but some were merchants and others were in the Roman Army.

Paul lived in a house that he had rented and was guarded by a soldier, who sat at the door or at the gate, as is the custom in the Near East when a political prisoner is under house arrest.

Paul was free to communicate with all the Jews in Rome and receive callers. It must be remembered that Paul, in the eyes of the Romans, was not a criminal. He was delivered to the Romans by Jewish authorities because of religious matters in which the Romans had no interest or concern. The Romans could even have helped Paul. (In the Near East during Dr. Lamsa's time, if a Christian should be imprisoned because of his controversial beliefs and delivered into a Muslim jail, the Muslims would assuredly be sympathetic toward him and vice versa.)

The Church in Rome was organized by Paul during the two years

---

[4]Acts 28:30-31, Aramaic Peshitta text, Lamsa translation.

of his imprisonment. The little lodging place he had rented was used as a meeting place. Although Paul was bound in chains, he was able to add new followers to the growing Christian movement in the Imperial City. During his confinement, Paul continually preached and taught the kingdom of God that Jesus had declared throughout Galilee and Judea.[5]

Tradition says that Paul was eventually freed from his house arrest and had left for Spain. There were many Jewish colonies in that country and it was Paul's custom to visit the Jewish communities that were scattered throughout the Roman Empire. He wanted to preach to them the gospel that Jesus taught. We learn about Paul's desire and plan to visit Spain from his epistle to the Romans,[6] but we know nothing more about him.

---

[5]Acts 28:30-31.
[6]Rom. 15:24-25.

BIBLIOGRAPHY

ARAMAIC AND SEMITIC STUDIES

Black, Matthew, *An Aramaic Approach to the Gospels and Acts*, Peabody, Mass., Hendrickson, Third edition, 1967 & 1998.

Burkert, Walter, *The Orientalizing Revolution*: *Near Eastern Influence on Greek Culture in the Early Archaic Age*, Harvard University Press, 1992.

Chilton, Bruce & Neusner, Jacob, *Judaism in the New Testament*, London, Routledge, 1995.

Eisenberg, Azriel, *The Synagogue through the Ages*, New York, Block Publishing Company, 1974.

Errico, Rocco A., *Setting A Trap For God*: *The Aramaic Prayer of Jesus*, Unity Village, Unity Books, 1997.
_____, *Let There Be Light*: *The Seven Keys*, Smyrna, GA, Noohra Foundation, 1994.
_____, *And There Was Light*, Smyrna, GA, Noohra Foundation, 1998.
_____, *The Mysteries of Creation*: *The Genesis Story*, Smyrna, GA, Noohra Foundation, 1993.
_____, *The Message of Matthew*: *An Annotated Parallel Aramaic-English Gospel of Matthew*, Smyrna, GA, Noohra Foundation, 1991.

Errico, Rocco A. & Lamsa, George M. *Aramaic Light on the Gospel of Matthew*, Smyrna, GA, Noohra Foundation, 2000.
_____, *Aramaic Light on the Gospels of Mark and Luke*, Smyrna, GA, Noohra Foundation, 2001.
_____, *Aramaic Light on the Gospel of John*, Smyrna, GA, Noohra Foundation, 2002.

Fitzmyer, Joseph, *A Wandering Aramean*: *A Collection of Aramaic Essays*, Chico, CA, Scholar Press, 1979.
_____, *Essays on the Semitic Background of the New Testament*, Chico, CA Scholar Press, 1974.

Hitti, Philip K., ***The Near East in History***, Princeton: D. Van Nostrand Co. 1960.

Lamsa, George M., ***The Oldest Christian People***, New York, Macmillan, 1926.

_____, ***My Neighbor Jesus***: *In the Light of His Own Language, People, and Time*, Philadelphia, A. J. Holman, 1932.

_____, ***New Testament Origin***, New York, Ziff Davis, 1947.

_____, ***The Kingdom on Earth***, Unity Village, Unity Books, 1966.

_____, ***The Holy Bible***: *From the Ancient Eastern Texts*, San Francisco, Harper Collins, (originally A. J. Holman) 1957.

Lawrence, T. E., ***Seven Pillars of Wisdom***, Garden City, New York, Doubleday, 1926.

McCullogh, W. Stewart, ***A Short History of Syriac Christianity to the Rise of Islam***, Chico, CA, Scholars Press, 1982.

Moffett, Samuel H., ***A History of Christianity in Asia***, Vol. 1, Harper, San Francisco, 1992.

Rihbany, Abraham M., ***The Syrian Christ***, Boston, Houghton Mifflin, 1916.

Wigram, W. A., ***The Assyrians and Their Neighbors***, London, G. Bell and Sons, 1929.

ABOUT THE AUTHOR
George M. Lamsa

George M. Lamsa, Th.D., a renowned native Assyrian scholar of the Holy Bible, translator, lecturer, ethnologist and author, was born August 5, 1892 in a civilization with customs, manners and language almost identical to those in the time of Jesus. His native tongue was full of similar idioms and parables, untouched by the outside world in 1900 years.

Until World War 1, his people living in that part of the ancient biblical lands that today is known as Kurdistan, in the basin of the rivers Tigris and Euphrates, retained the simple nomadic life as in the days of the Hebrew patriarchs. Only at the beginning of the 20th century did the isolated segment of the once great Assyrian Empire learn of the discovery of America and the Reformation in Germany.

Likewise, until that same time, this ancient culture of early Christians was unknown to the Western world, and the Aramaic language was thought to be dead. But in this so-called "Cradle of Civilization," primitive biblical customs and Semitic culture, cut off from the world, were preserved.

Lamsa's primary upbringing as a boy was to tend the lambs. But, as the first-born in his family, while yet an infant he was dedicated to God by his devout mother. Years after her death, when Lamsa was 12 years of age, her vow was renewed by native tribesmen, an ox killed and its blood rubbed on his forehead. Lamsa claimed this vow to God had always been part of him. "God's hand," he affirmed, "has been steadfastly on my shoulder, guiding me in the divine work."

Lamsa's formal education and studies began under the priests and deacons of the ancient Church of the East. Later he graduated with the highest honors ever bestowed from the Archbishop of Canterbury's Colleges in Iran and in Turkey, with the degree of Bachelor of Arts. Lamsa never married, but dedicated his life to "God's calling." He spoke eight languages and his lowest grade in any subject was 99.

At the beginning of World War 1, when Turkey began its

invasions, Lamsa was forced to flee the Imperial University at Constantinople where he was studying. He went to South America where he endured great hardships during those years. He knew but three words in Spanish at that time—water, work and bread. As best as he could he existed—in the British Merchant Marine for a time, then working on railroads, in mines and later in printing shops, a trade he had learned while attending college in Iran.

After arriving in the United States in his early 20s, Lamsa worked by day as a printer, and by night he went to school. He later studied at the Episcopal Theological Seminary in Alexandria, Virginia, and at Dropsie College in Philadelphia.

It was through his struggles, during these years, with the English idioms that Lamsa gradually launched into his "life's work" of translating the Holy Bible from Aramaic into English. Yet many years were to pass before the world received his translations.

First as a lecturer in churches and seminaries, in halls and auditoriums, before statesmen, theologians, groups of artists, actors and others, Lamsa received recognition as a poet-philosopher and as an authority on all phases of Near Eastern civilization.

It was his own inner compulsion, and the urging of hundreds who heard him, that drove him forward and brought about—after 30 years of labor, research and study—his translation of the Holy Bible from a branch of the ancient Aramaic language that the earliest Christians used. (It is a know fact that Jesus and his followers spoke Aramaic.)

There were times that he was temporarily stopped in his translations when the idioms in the manuscripts could not be given correct English equivalents. It was Lamsa's firm belief that his translation from Aramaic would bring people closer to the Word of God and would facilitate understanding between the East and the West. For forty years, he produced commentaries and many other works based on the Aramaic language. The last ten years of his life, Dr. Lamsa tutored and prepared Dr. Rocco A. Errico to continue with the Aramaic approach to Scripture. He left this earthly life on September 22, 1975, in Turlock, California.

ABOUT THE AUTHOR
Rocco A. Errico

Dr. Rocco A. Errico is an ordained minister, international lecturer and author, spiritual counselor, and one of the nation's leading Biblical scholars working from the original Aramaic *Peshitta* texts. For ten years he studied intensively with Dr. George M. Lamsa, Th.D., (1890-1975), world-renowned Assyrian biblical scholar and translator of the *Holy Bible from the Ancient Eastern Text.* Dr. Errico is proficient in Aramaic and Hebrew exegesis, helping thousands of readers and seminar participants understand how the Semitic context of culture, language, idioms, symbolism, mystical style, psychology, and literary amplification—the *Seven Keys* that unlock the Bible—are essential to understanding this ancient spiritual document.

Dr. Errico is the recipient of numerous awards and academic degrees, including a Doctorate in Philosophy from the School of Christianity in Los Angeles; a Doctorate in Divinity from St. Ephrem's Institute in Sweden; and a Doctorate in Sacred Theology from the School of Christianity in Los Angeles. In 1993, the American Apostolic University College of Seminarians awarded him a Doctorate of Letters. He also holds a special title of Teacher, Prime Exegete, *Maplana d'miltha dalaha*, among the Federation of St. Thomas Christians of the order of Antioch.

Dr. Errico is a featured speaker at conferences, symposia, and seminars throughout the United States, Canada, Mexico and Europe and has been a regular contributor for over 23 years to *Science of Mind Magazine* (circulation: 150,000), a monthly journal founded in 1872. He began his practice as an ordained minister and pastoral counselor in the mid-1950s and during the next three decades served in churches and missions in Missouri, Texas, Mexico, and California. Throughout his public work, Dr. Errico has stressed the nonsectarian, *open* interpretation of Biblical spirituality, prying it free from 2000 years of rigid orthodoxy, which, according to his research, is founded on incorrect translations of the original Aramaic texts.

In 1970, Dr. Errico established the Noohra Foundation in San Antonio, Texas, as a non-profit, non-sectarian spiritual-educational organization devoted to helping people of all faiths to understand the Near Eastern background and Aramaic interpretation of the Bible. In 1976, Dr. Errico relocated the Noohra Foundation in Irvine, California, where it flourished for the next 17 years. For seven years, the Noohra Foundation operated in Santa Fe, New Mexico, and in September 2001, it relocated to Smyrna, Georgia, where Dr. Errico is Dean of Biblical Studies for Dr. Barbara King's School of Ministry—Hillside Chapel and Truth Center.

Under the auspices of the Noohra Foundation, Dr. Errico continues to lecture for colleges, civic groups and churches of various denominations in the United States, Canada, Mexico and Europe.

For a complimentary catalog of Aramaic Bible translations, books, audio and video cassettes, and a brochure of classes, retreats and seminars, or for any other inquiries, write or call the Noohra Foundation. Those interested in scheduling Dr. Errico for a personal appearance may also contact:

Noohra Foundation
PMB 343
4480H South Cobb Drive
Smyrna, GA 30080

Phone: 770-319-9376
Fax: 770-319-9793

E-mail: noohrafnd@aol.com

Noohra Foundation web-site: www.noohra.com

In addition to *Aramaic Light on the Acts of the Apostles*, the Noohra Foundation is pleased to offer the following books and commentaries by Dr. Rocco A. Errico and Dr. George M. Lamsa.

Commentaries by Dr. Errico and Dr. Lamsa

ARAMAIC LIGHT ON THE GOSPEL OF MATTHEW
(Aramaic New Testament Series Volume 1)

This inimitable commentary acts as a Near Eastern guide, taking you through the heart of the gospels, illuminating difficult and puzzling passages and offering unparalleled insight into the character and behavior of Near Eastern Semites. This volume is more than just a revision of Dr. Lamsa's commentaries, *Gospel Light* and *More Light on the Gospels*. Dr. Errico has edited, expanded and annotated these previous works and added unpublished material that the two of them had drafted just before Dr. Lamsa died in 1975. Dr. Errico completed the comments that they had only outlined and also included information derived from his continual research in Aramaic word meanings and Near Eastern Semitic Studies. $29.95

ARAMAIC LIGHT ON THE GOSPELS OF MARK AND LUKE
(Aramaic New Testament Series Volume 2)

Like the previous volume, this commentary carries you back almost two thousand years, providing a clear perspective of Jesus in the light of his own language, people and times. However, this volume is unique in that it provides insight into the psychology of Jesus' healing methods. $26.95

ARAMAIC LIGHT ON THE GOSPEL OF JOHN
(Aramaic New Testament Series Volume 3)

Dr. Errico and Dr. Lamsa bring clarity and understanding to the most popular (and most misunderstood) gospel. In the 3rd volume of this series, you will learn the Semitic meanings behind such terms as "the

Word," "Light," "Life," "Christ," "Only Begotten." You will also come to understand what Jesus meant when he said "No man comes to the Father except through me" and many other sayings that appear to be sectarian and exclusive. $26.95

Books by Dr. Errico:

LET THERE BE LIGHT: THE SEVEN KEYS

The Bible is more than anything else a Near Eastern account of spiritual events and teachings. In this illuminating work, Dr. Errico builds a bridge between Western ways of understanding and the Near Eastern social realities that are embedded in the Bible. He helps us to see the Bible through Semitic, Aramaic eyes. Bypassing doctrinal creeds and rigid interpretations, he corrects numerous errors and misleading literal translations that have caused confusion for centuries. This book equips the reader with seven key insights to understand the allusions, parables, and teachings of the Bible, opening the door to the ancient Aramaic world from which the Bible emerged. $17.95

AND THERE WAS LIGHT

Like its predecessor *Let There Be Light*, this books takes us through the heart of the Hebrew Bible and New Testament by working with Aramaic—the language spoken by the Patriarchs, Jesus, his apostles and their contemporaries. With his knowledge of the customs, idioms, psychology, symbolism and philosophy of Semitic peoples, Dr. Errico unlocks puzzling passages. Suddenly the Bible, from Genesis to Revelation, becomes clearer and more relevant for Western readers. The teaching ministry and parables of Jesus come alive as you've never read before. Topics include: *Rabbi Eshoa-Jesus—An Aramaic Speaking Shemite, Uncovering Jesus' Gospel, The Parables of Jesus (Dr. Errico's translation), Perfect Love, An Expanded Teaching on the 23rd Psalm, The Book of the Revelation.*
$19.95

SETTING A TRAP FOR GOD: The Aramaic Prayer of Jesus

A revised and expanded version of Dr. Errico's most popular book—his translation (with commentary) of the Lord's Prayer. Using his own translation directly from the original Aramaic source, Dr. Errico interprets the prayer in terms of eight attunements that align us to spiritual forces in and around us, which is precisely how Jesus taught his disciples to tune in to the inexhaustible power of the Heavenly Father. What exactly does the word "prayer" mean? What does it accomplish? Dr. Errico focuses on original Aramaic manuscripts and the ancient culture of the Near East as he answers these questions. Discover the way of peace, health, and prosperity as you learn to "set a trap" for the inexhaustible power of God. $10.95

THE MYSTERIES OF CREATION: The Genesis Story

A challenging new look at the processes and mysteries of the primal creation account. Dr. Errico uses his own direct translation from the Aramaic-Peshitta text of Genesis 1:1-31 and 2:103. He discusses the Semitic meaning, names and theories of the origin of God. Where appropriate, Dr. Errico borrows insights from the world of both quantum physics and biblical scholarship. He shows readers that behind the material appearance of the world operates a sacred intelligence (called *Elohim*) and that all creation is a meaningful representation of the creative acts of this primal deity. *The Genesis Story* introduces to humankind its responsibility to the earth and its environment. $16.95

THE MESSAGE OF MATTHEW: An Annotated Parallel Aramaic-English Gospel of Matthew

Dr. Errico's stirring translation of the ancient Aramaic Peshitta text of Matthew is further enriched with his stimulating and illuminating annotations. The style of writing in *The Message of Matthew* is simple and direct. The English translation is printed on the left side of the page with footnotes. The Aramaic text is printed on the right with additional footnotes in English. These valuable footnotes explain the meanings of Aramaic words and customs with supplementary historical information. $24.95

CLASSICAL ARAMAIC: Book I (with Father Michael Bazzi)

Learn to read and write the language of Jesus in a self-teachable format. Classical Aramaic is a practical grammar that prepares you to read the New Testament in Jesus' own native tongue. $24.95

LA ANTIGUA ORACIÓN ARAMEA DE JESÚS: El Padrenuestro

Dr. Errico's own translation into Spanish of his book *The Ancient Aramaic Prayer of Jesus*. $8.95

ACHT EINSTIMMUNGEN AUF GOTT: Vaterunser

German translation and publication of Dr. Errico's book *Setting a Trap for God*.

ES WERDE LICHT

German translation and publication of Dr. Errico's book *Let There Be Light: The Seven Keys*.

Books by Dr. Lamsa

THE HOLY BIBLE FROM THE ANCIENT EASTERN TEXT

The entire Bible translated directly into English from Aramaic, the language of Jesus. There are approximately 12,000 major differences between this English translation and the many traditional versions of the Bible. One example: "For I the Lord thy God am a *jealous* God." (Exodus 20:5 King James Version) "For I the Lord your God am a *zealous* God." (Lamsa translation) Another example: "And *lead us* not into temptation..." (Matthew 6:13 KJV) "And *do not let us* enter into temptation... (Lamsa translation). $35.00

IDIOMS IN THE BIBLE EXPLAINED and A KEY TO THE ORIGINAL GOSPELS

Two books in one. In Book 1 (*Idioms in the Bible Explained*) Dr. Lamsa explains nearly 1000 crucial idioms and colloquialisms of Eastern speech that will enrich reading of the Old and New Testaments for student and general reader alike. Obscure and difficult biblical passages are listed and compared with the King James Version. These make clear the original meaning of such ancient idioms and assure that our grasp of the biblical message is more sound and rewarding. Example: "Lot's wife became a pillar of salt" means she suffered a stroke, became paralyzed and died.

Book 2 (*A Key to the Original Gospels*) explains how the gospels were written, the reason for two different genealogies, the conflicting stories of the birth of Jesus, and more. $14.00

THE KINGDOM ON EARTH

Part One—The Beatitudes, Part Two—The Lord's Prayer. Many scholars and teachers have dealt with the Sermon on the Mount, which has been called the "constitution of the Kingdom of heaven." None is more eminently qualified than Dr. Lamsa because no one else with his background has a similar knowledge of the Bible and of biblical times. With a warmth and understanding seldom equaled among contemporary scholars, Dr. Lamsa teaches the Beatitudes and the Lord's prayer in the light of Jesus' own language, people and times. $14.95

THE SHEPHERD OF ALL: The Twenty-Third Psalm

The Twenty-third Psalm, considered by many to be the most meaningful psalm in the Bible, is brought to life in a most vivid manner. Dr. Lamsa's ancestors for untold generations were sheep raising people and he was raised in a sheep camp. Based on his own personal experience as a shepherd, Dr. Lamsa interprets this beautiful and moving psalm in the light of Eastern biblical customs. $5.95

NEW TESTAMENT ORIGIN

Dr. Lamsa presents his theory for Aramaic as the original written language of the New Testament. To quote Dr. Lamsa in the forward of *New Testament Origin*: "The Aramaic text speaks for itself; it needs no defense. It is strongly supported by internal evidence, by the Aramaic style of writing, idioms, metaphors, and Oriental [Semitic] mannerisms of speech. Since Christianity is an Eastern religion, the Scriptures must have been written in an Eastern tongue. This fact will be recognized easily by any philologist familiar with Semitic languages. I am one of the millions in biblical lands—both Christians and Mohammedans—who believe that the New Testament was first written in Aramaic, and that our texts were carefully handed down from apostolic times." $5.95

AN HOUR WITH DR. GEORGE M. LAMSA (VIDEO)

Originally taped for TV in 1972 in Cadillac, Michigan under the title Lamsa at His Best. With the kind permission of Dr. Lamsa's family, we are now able to share this rare event in VHS format. A wonderful opportunity to see and hear Dr. Lamsa "live" as he answers many questions on the Bible from the Aramaic perspective. $29.95

Dr. Errico Audio Tapes

Below is a sampling of titles of audio tapes from classes, seminars, and Sunday talks given by Dr. Errico:

The Lord's Prayer in Aramaic	The Tree of Good & Evil
Jesus' Healing Methods	Jesus' Birth & Genealogy
The Kingdom or the Cross?	Mystery of the Resurrection
Book of the Revelation	Passion Week of Christ
The Great Shepherd	The Mysteries of Creation
Dreams and Visions	God, Sexuality & the Bible
Self-Compassion	The Devil

Moses: Liberator, Revelator, Terminator, Magician

NOTES

NOTES

NOTES

NOTES

NOTES

NOTES